I would like to dedicate this book to my beloved wife, my parents, my sibilings, my children, my business assistance & All Construction Industry experts, who brought Indian construction industry to this glorious stage.

# INTEGRATING MEPF AND ARCHITECTURAL DESIGN FOR SMARTER BUILDINGS

## CHOOSE YOUR RIGHT DESIGN PARTNER

ALTAF ABDUL

# Contents

# Preface

**About Author:**

Altaf Abdul is the Principal Consultant at A-Square MEP Consultants, a leading firm based in Bengaluru, Karnataka, specializing in Mechanical, Electrical, and Plumbing (MEP) engineering services. With over two decades of experience in the industry, Altaf has established himself as a prominent figure in the MEP consulting domain, known for his technical expertise, innovative solutions, and commitment to excellence.

**Early Career and Educational Background**

Altaf Abdul's journey in the MEP industry began with a solid educational foundation in engineering. He pursued his studies with a focus on electrical and mechanical systems, equipping him with the knowledge necessary to understand the intricacies of building services. His passion for engineering and problem-solving led him to specialize in MEP systems, where he found his true calling.

Early in his career, Altaf worked with various organizations, gaining hands-on experience in designing, implementing, and managing MEP systems across different sectors. This exposure allowed him to develop a comprehensive understanding of the challenges and requirements associated with MEP engineering, laying the groundwork for his future endeavours.

**Founding A-Square MEP Consultants**

In 2004, Altaf founded A-Square MEP Consultants with the vision of providing innovative and sustainable MEP solutions to clients. Under his leadership, the firm has grown to become one of the most respected MEP consulting companies in Bengaluru, known for its commitment to quality and client satisfaction.

A-Square MEP Consultants offers a range of services, including engineering design and technical audits. The firm's expertise spans various industries, such as commercial, residential, industrial, and institutional projects. Altaf's hands-on approach and attention to detail have been instrumental in the firm's success, ensuring that each project is executed to the highest standards.

**Technical Expertise and Contributions**

Altaf Abdul possesses extensive experience in various MEP systems, including electrical, plumbing, air-conditioning, fire alarm systems, fire suppression systems, data networking, and security systems. His expertise extends to industrial applications, where he has been involved in designing and implementing complex MEP systems tailored to the specific needs of manufacturing facilities.

Beyond his consulting work, Altaf is an active contributor to the engineering community. He regularly shares his insights and knowledge through articles and posts on platforms like LinkedIn, discussing topics such as HVAC system design, energy efficiency, and the role of MEP consultants in building infrastructure. His thought leadership has garnered a following among industry professionals seeking to stay informed about the latest trends and best practices in MEP engineering.

**Client-Centric Approach and Project Highlights**

A hallmark of Altaf's leadership is his client-centric approach. He believes in building strong, long-term relationships with clients by understanding their unique requirements and delivering solutions that exceed expectations. This philosophy has led to numerous successful projects and repeat business from satisfied clients.

Notable projects under Altaf's guidance include the design and implementation of MEP systems for commercial complexes, educational institutions, data centres, and manufacturing plants. Each project reflects his commitment to quality, sustainability, and innovation.

**Vision for the Future**

Looking ahead, Altaf Abdul aims to continue expanding A-Square MEP Consultants' reach, both within India and internationally. He envisions the firm becoming a global leader in MEP consulting, known for its innovative solutions and commitment to excellence. To achieve this, Altaf plans to invest in research and development, embrace emerging technologies, and foster a culture of continuous learning within the organization.

In summary, Altaf Abdul's journey from an aspiring engineer to the Principal Consultant of a leading MEP consulting firm is a testament to his dedication, expertise, and vision. Through his leadership, A-Square MEP Consultants continues to set new standards in the industry, delivering high-quality, sustainable, and innovative MEP solutions to clients across various sectors.

# Synopsis Of "design Synergy: Integrating Mepf And Architecture For Smarter Buildings"

**"Design Synergy: Integrating MEPF and Architecture for Smarter Buildings"** is a comprehensive exploration of how **Mechanical, Electrical, Plumbing (MEPF)** systems can be successfully integrated with architectural design principles to create high-performance, sustainable, and smart buildings. This book is geared toward professionals in architecture, engineering, and construction, focusing on the vital role that early collaboration and cutting-edge technology play in improving the design, construction, and operation of modern buildings.

The book is structured into **15 chapters**, each addressing a different facet of integrated design and the key challenges and benefits associated with combining MEPF systems with architectural design to create smarter, more sustainable buildings.

**Part 1: Foundations of Integrated Design**

The first part of the book sets the stage for understanding the principles behind **integrated design** and the significance of collaboration between **architects** and **MEPF engineers**.

**Chapter 1: Introduction to Integrated Building Design**

This chapter introduces the concept of **integrated building design**, emphasizing the importance of collaboration among all disciplines—**architecture, MEPF systems, structural engineering**, and **construction management**. It underscores the profound impact that collaboration can have on improving **energy efficiency**, reducing operational costs, enhancing sustainability, and ultimately improving building performance. The chapter also highlights how integrated design leads to the creation of **smarter buildings** that can adapt to changing environmental conditions, enhance occupant comfort, and optimize energy consumption.

**Chapter 2: Understanding Architectural Design Principles**

This chapter explains core architectural principles such as **space planning, aesthetics**, and **user experience**. It explores the **form vs. function debate** and how integrated design can bridge the gap between artistic vision and practical functionality. The architectural design process is discussed in relation to how architects consider structural requirements and space utilization while creating buildings that are visually appealing, functional, and sustainable.

## Chapter 3: Fundamentals of MEPF Systems

In this chapter, readers gain an understanding of **MEPF systems**, which include **mechanical, electrical**, and **plumbing** systems. It delves into how these systems support the operation of a building, from heating, ventilation, and air conditioning (HVAC) to **electrical distribution** and **water management**. It also addresses the interdependence of these systems and the importance of their seamless integration with architectural elements to create efficient and sustainable buildings.

## Part 2: The Need for Integration

The second part of the book focuses on the necessity of **integrating MEPF systems with architectural design** to overcome traditional silos and enhance building performance.

## Chapter 4: Challenges in Traditional Design Approach

This chapter analyses the traditional design approach, where architecture, MEPF systems, and structural engineering are often considered separately, leading to design conflicts, rework, and inefficiencies. It identifies specific challenges such as **siloed working methods, clash detection** issues, and the inefficiencies that arise from disconnected design processes.

## Chapter 5: Benefits of Integrated Design

Here, the book discusses the **benefits of integrated design** in detail. By encouraging collaboration from the beginning, integrated design leads to **energy efficiency, cost savings**, and enhanced **functional performance**. This chapter highlights how integrated design improves the coordination between systems, reduces rework, and increases the overall quality of the project. The chapter also covers the importance of **sustainability**, which can be achieved through collaborative efforts between architects and MEPF engineers.

## Chapter 6: Codes, Standards, and Compliance

This chapter emphasizes the role of building codes and standards in the design and construction of buildings. It discusses the importance of adhering to national and international building codes such as **ASHRAE, National Electrical Code (NEC)**, and the **National Building Code (NBC)**, and how these codes shape the design of MEPF systems. The chapter underscores the need for interdisciplinary coordination to meet compliance requirements, ensuring that buildings are both safe and functional.

## Part 3: Integration Strategies

The third part of the book focuses on practical strategies for integrating MEPF systems with architecture during the design phase.

**Chapter 7: Early Stage Collaboration**

This chapter discusses the importance of involving MEPF engineers early in the design process to create a fully integrated building system. **Design charrettes**, where all team members collaborate from the beginning, are highlighted as a critical tool for fostering communication, aligning goals, and solving problems early. The chapter stresses that early collaboration ensures the systems can be integrated without conflicts, leading to a more efficient design and construction process.

**Chapter 8: Building Information Modelling (BIM)**

Building Information Modelling (BIM) is discussed as a **revolutionary tool** for enhancing integration in the design process. BIM enables **3D modelling** that allows architects, MEPF engineers, and other stakeholders to work from a shared model, improving coordination and reducing design conflicts. This chapter explores BIM's role in **clash detection, real-time collaboration**, and **system simulation** to ensure that systems such as HVAC, electrical, and plumbing are seamlessly integrated from the outset.

**Chapter 9: Design Workflows and Coordination Tools**

This chapter explores the tools and workflows that facilitate **real-time coordination** between design teams. It focuses on the **software tools** like **Revit, Navisworks**, and **AutoCAD MEPF**, and their role in streamlining design workflows and improving coordination among different teams. It also discusses **cloud-based platforms** that support real-time collaboration, providing project teams with the tools to work more efficiently and stay aligned throughout the design process.

**Part 4: Real-World Applications**

The fourth part of the book focuses on real-world case studies and examples of successful integrated design.

**Chapter 10: Case Studies of Successful Integration**

This chapter provides in-depth case studies of buildings where **integrated design** has been successfully applied. It showcases **real-world projects** (commercial, residential, and institutional) that benefited from early collaboration between architects and MEPF engineers. Key lessons learned and best practices are shared from each case, demonstrating how integrated design can result in **cost savings, increased energy efficiency, and improved occupant comfort.**

**Chapter 11: Sustainability and Green Building Certifications**

Focusing on sustainability, this chapter explores how integrated design supports green building certifications such as **LEED, BREEAM, IGBC** and **GRIHA**. It discusses the role of architects and MEPF engineers in achieving sustainability goals through the integration of energy-efficient systems, renewable energy sources, and sustainable materials. The chapter also covers how integrated design helps buildings meet the stringent criteria for green building certifications, promoting **environmental responsibility** and **long-term savings**.

### Chapter 12: Smart Buildings and Emerging Technologies

As technology continues to evolve, this chapter discusses how **smart buildings** are changing the way MEPF systems are integrated with architecture. The integration of **IoT, AI**, and **sensors** into building systems allows for real-time data monitoring, optimization, and automation. The chapter explores how emerging technologies contribute to building performance, improving **energy efficiency, occupant comfort**, and **sustainability**.

### Part 5: Execution and Management

The final part of the book focuses on **execution, project management**, and the importance of **coordination techniques** in ensuring successful project delivery.

### Chapter 13: Project Management and Coordination Techniques

This chapter delves into the **project management** techniques used to ensure that all stakeholders are aligned and that the project stays on schedule and within budget. It covers key elements of successful project management, including **coordination meetings, real-time collaboration, RFIs (Requests for Information)**, and **managing scope creep**. Effective project management ensures that the building systems are properly integrated, tested, and commissioned on time.

### Chapter 14: Quality Control and Commissioning

Focusing on the critical phase of **quality control** and **commissioning**, this chapter examines the testing and verification processes that ensure building systems perform as designed. It discusses how commissioning verifies the functionality of MEPF systems, identifies potential issues before occupancy, and ensures compliance with building codes and regulations. **Final walkthroughs** and **system optimization** are also covered as part of the commissioning process.

### Chapter 15: The Future of Integrated Design

The concluding chapter explores the future of integrated design in the context of **emerging technologies** and **sustainability goals**. It discusses the role of **AI**, **automation**, and **prefabrication** in streamlining the design and construction processes, as well as the growing importance of **smart buildings**. The chapter also looks at how integrated design will continue to evolve in response to environmental challenges, energy demands, and technological advances, ensuring that future buildings are more **resilient**, **efficient**, and **sustainable**.

**Conclusion**

"**Design Synergy: Integrating MEPF and Architecture for Smarter Buildings**" offers a comprehensive look at how the collaboration between architects, MEPF engineers, and other stakeholders leads to the creation of high-performance, energy-efficient, and sustainable buildings. By integrating modern tools such as BIM, AI, and IoT into the design process, the book demonstrates how these technologies improve building systems, enhance occupant comfort, and reduce operational costs.

With **real-world case studies**, practical tips for **project management**, and a thorough exploration of the role of **sustainability** and **green building certifications**, the book serves as an essential guide for professionals seeking to understand and implement **integrated design** in the modern construction industry. As the industry continues to evolve, the integration of architecture and MEPF systems will play a pivotal role in shaping the future of smarter, more sustainable buildings.

# CHAPTER ONE

# Introduction to Integrated Building Design

**1.1 Importance of Collaboration**

In the rapidly evolving world of construction, the design of modern buildings has become a complex and multidisciplinary endeavour. Traditional practices, where architects and engineers worked in isolated silos, have given way to more integrated approaches that encourage communication, cooperation, and shared problem-solving. Integrated building design (IBD) involves a collaborative effort between architects, engineers, contractors, and other key stakeholders to create a unified vision for the building from conception through to its operation.

The importance of collaboration cannot be overstated. It allows for the seamless integration of various building systems, such as mechanical, electrical, plumbing (MEPF), and architectural elements. Each of these systems plays a vital role in the building's overall functionality, comfort, and performance. However, without effective communication and coordination between these disciplines, designs can conflict, resulting in costly delays, increased rework, and suboptimal building performance.

In an integrated design process, all stakeholders are involved early in the planning stages, which facilitates more informed decision-making. The result is a building that is better aligned with its functional goals, meets sustainability targets, is more energy-efficient, and is often more cost-effective than buildings designed through traditional, siloed methods.

**1.2 Impact on Sustainability, Efficiency, Cost, and Performance**

The modern building sector is under increasing pressure to reduce its environmental impact, lower operating costs, and provide higher performance in terms of occupant comfort and usability. Integrated design directly supports these objectives, particularly in the areas of sustainability, operational efficiency, cost savings, and overall building performance.

**Sustainability**: One of the primary goals of integrated design is the creation of energy-efficient buildings that reduce resource consumption and minimize environmental impact. By optimizing the interactions between architectural and MEPF systems, integrated design helps reduce the need for energy-intensive systems like heating, cooling, and artificial lighting. This is especially important as the building sector is responsible for a significant portion of global greenhouse gas emissions. Integrated design practices can incorporate renewable energy systems, efficient HVAC systems, and high-performance building envelopes that contribute to energy savings and support certifications like LEED, IGBC, or GRIHA.

**Efficiency**: Integrated design ensures that all systems within the building work together harmoniously, leading to improved efficiency. For example, a well-coordinated MEPF system ensures that the heating, cooling, and electrical systems are appropriately sized, reducing energy wastage and optimizing overall building performance. A key component of efficiency is also operational cost reduction, as buildings with optimized systems require less maintenance and lower energy use.

**Cost Savings**: While integrated design may initially require higher upfront investment due to the time and resources spent on coordination, the long-term cost savings can be substantial. By addressing potential issues early in the design phase, integrated teams reduce the risk of costly changes and redesigns later in the project. Furthermore, the improved energy efficiency and reduced operational costs of the building can result in significant savings over the building's lifespan. This is particularly true in the case of buildings aiming for high sustainability ratings, as they often enjoy financial benefits through tax incentives, energy rebates, and higher market value.

**Performance**: A building that is designed with integration in mind not only performs better but also offers a higher level of comfort to its occupants. Coordinated design efforts result in better lighting, air quality, temperature control, and noise reduction. When MEPF systems are integrated effectively with architectural design, they create a more comfortable environment by ensuring that all systems are designed to support the needs of the users without competing or creating unnecessary complexity.

Moreover, integrated design fosters innovation. The collaborative approach encourages stakeholders to push the boundaries of what is possible by sharing insights and expertise from various disciplines. This leads to creative solutions that address both aesthetic and functional challenges in new and exciting ways.

### 1.3 The Role of Technology in Integrated Design

Technology plays a critical role in the success of integrated building design. Advances in Building Information Modelling (BIM), 3D simulations, and real-time collaboration platforms have transformed how architects, engineers, and contractors collaborate. These tools enable design teams to work together efficiently, making it easier to visualize, simulate, and optimize the entire building system before construction begins.

BIM has revolutionized the industry by creating a digital representation of the physical and functional characteristics of a building. This digital model provides all team members with access to real-time data and insights, facilitating smoother coordination and reducing the chances of miscommunication. For example, architects can visualize the layout and size of HVAC ducts in relation to the building's layout and aesthetic design, while engineers can assess how the placement of windows and doors affects the building's energy performance.

Additionally, technologies like artificial intelligence (AI) and machine learning (ML) are being used to optimize building designs, improve decision-making, and predict long-term performance. For example, AI can help automate energy modeling, providing real-time data on energy consumption patterns and helping design teams make informed decisions to reduce energy use.

### 1.4 The Benefits of an Integrated Approach to Building Design

Integrated design brings many advantages to building projects, benefiting not only the building's owners and occupants but also the broader community. Some of the key benefits include:

1. **Faster Time-to-Market**: With all stakeholders involved from the beginning, the design process is streamlined, reducing the time required for design revisions and approvals. This means that buildings can be completed faster, meeting the demands of the project timeline without compromising on quality.

2. **Enhanced Innovation**: Collaboration between architects and engineers allows for the exchange of ideas that would not have been possible in traditional silos. This cross-pollination of expertise fosters innovation and results in more creative, efficient, and functional building solutions.

3. **Holistic Approach**: Integrated design allows for a more holistic approach to problem-solving, where all systems—architecture, MEPF, and even landscaping—are considered in relation to one another. This ensures that each decision supports the overall goals of the building, whether that be sustainability, user experience, or operational efficiency.

4. **Better Risk Management**: When design teams are well-integrated, the risk of miscommunication or oversight is minimized. Additionally, the early identification of potential conflicts or challenges allows teams to devise solutions proactively, rather than reacting to problems that arise later in the process.

5. **Increased Client Satisfaction**: Finally, integrated design results in buildings that better meet the needs of the client. Whether the building's purpose is residential, commercial, or institutional, an integrated approach ensures that all systems function together to create a cohesive, efficient, and user-friendly environment.

**Conclusion**

As we enter an era of increasingly complex and resource-conscious building design, integrated design practices are more important than ever. By fostering collaboration between architects, engineers, and other stakeholders, integrated design ensures that buildings not only meet their functional requirements but also contribute positively to the environment and the community. The integration of MEPF systems with architectural design is no longer just a best practice but a necessity for creating smarter, more sustainable buildings that can perform efficiently throughout their lifespan.

# CHAPTER TWO

# Understanding Architectural Design Principles

**Space Planning, Aesthetics, and User Experience**

Architectural design is fundamentally concerned with creating spaces that are functional, aesthetic, and conducive to a positive user experience. At the core of any architectural project is **space planning**, which involves organizing the physical layout of spaces within a building to ensure both efficiency and comfort. Good space planning considers how spaces will be used, how people will interact within them, and how various functions of the building can flow seamlessly.

Space planning goes beyond just placing rooms or walls; it focuses on how users will interact with the building's interior. Architects must consider factors such as **traffic flow**, accessibility, lighting, acoustics, and privacy. For example, in a commercial office building, an open-plan design may encourage collaboration, but this must be balanced with quiet areas for focused work. Similarly, in residential designs, architects must carefully arrange spaces for privacy, family interactions, and leisure.

**Aesthetics**, or the visual appeal of a building, is another important aspect of architectural design. Aesthetic considerations go beyond mere beauty and extend to how a building's design contributes to its environment. An architect's choice of materials, shapes, colours, and textures directly impacts the look and feel of the building. Aesthetic elements must also align with the function of the building. For example, in a healthcare facility, an architect might use calming colours and natural light to create a healing environment.

In the context of integrated design, aesthetics must also work in harmony with the MEPF systems. For instance, the positioning of ductwork, air vents, light fixtures, and power outlets should not interfere with the architectural vision. Integrating these systems early on in the design process allows for creative solutions that satisfy both functional and aesthetic requirements. Properly coordinated designs ensure that technical systems do not detract from the building's overall look, which is vital in spaces such as commercial offices, residential homes, and public buildings.

Ultimately, **user experience** is the most important metric of a building's success. The design should cater to the needs and behaviours of its occupants, enhancing comfort, safety, and accessibility. Architects carefully consider factors such as lighting, air quality, acoustic performance, thermal comfort, and spatial arrangement. A well-designed building supports a pleasant user experience by anticipating needs and providing solutions that improve daily life.

In integrated design, architects must collaborate with MEPF engineers to enhance the user experience. For example, natural ventilation and lighting can be maximized through strategic architectural decisions, and MEPF systems such as air conditioning or heating can be designed to complement these choices.

### Form vs Function Debate

The **form versus function** debate is one of the most enduring philosophical discussions in architecture. On one side, form refers to the aesthetic qualities of the building—the shapes, lines, and appearance that contribute to its overall visual appeal. Function, on the other hand, refers to the practical utility of the building—the way it supports its users' needs, provides comfort, and serves its purpose.

Historically, there has been a tension between these two aspects of design. Early 20th-century modernists, such as Le Corbusier and Frank Lloyd Wright, were proponents of the idea that form should follow function. For these architects, the primary goal of design was to meet the functional needs of the building's occupants, and aesthetic considerations should flow naturally from those needs. For example, Wright's famous Fallingwater residence was designed to integrate the natural landscape into the house's structure, reflecting a strong relationship between form and function.

However, over time, architecture has evolved to recognize that both form and function are essential to a building's success. Modern architecture embraces the notion that while functionality is paramount, aesthetic considerations should not be sacrificed. Today, architects seek to find a balance where the building's form enhances its function without compromising its visual appeal.

In integrated design, the form vs. function debate becomes particularly relevant. MEPF systems, which often involve complex technical components, must be designed in a way that complements the architectural form while maintaining functionality. For example, HVAC systems need to be efficient, but their design must also consider the architectural aesthetic of the building. Ductwork, pipes, and wiring must be hidden or integrated into the structure so that they do not detract from the building's overall design.

One of the goals of integrated design is to merge these two concerns—functionality and aesthetic appeal—by involving MEPF engineers in the design process from the outset. This allows for better alignment between the building's form and the functionality of its systems. When architects and MEPF engineers work together, they can explore innovative solutions that satisfy both the functional and visual requirements of the building. For instance, the use of concealed or innovative architectural solutions for MEPF systems—such as ceiling voids, raised floors, and decorative elements that also house lighting or HVAC systems—can create a seamless blend of form and function.

This partnership leads to buildings that not only serve their intended purpose efficiently but also provide an environment that delights the senses and meets the emotional and psychological needs of its users.

**Impact of Architecture on MEPF Integration**

Architectural design plays a crucial role in how MEPF systems are integrated into a building. The building's form—its shape, layout, and design decisions—directly affects how easily MEPF systems can be accommodated within the structure. Early collaboration between architects and MEPF engineers allows for solutions that meet both architectural goals and engineering constraints, ultimately improving the performance of the building's systems.

For example, when designing a building's HVAC system, the architect's decision regarding the ceiling height and space usage can greatly impact the placement and size of ducts. In a modern open-plan office space, higher ceilings may provide more flexibility in placing ducts, while in a compact residential apartment, engineers may need to find creative solutions to fit HVAC components without compromising comfort.

Similarly, the architect's consideration of natural light and ventilation influences the design of electrical and plumbing systems. The placement of windows, the building's orientation, and the integration of natural ventilation all affect the type and quantity of lighting, power outlets, and air handling systems needed to meet the building's environmental goals.

In an integrated design process, architects and MEPF engineers work together to address these challenges in the early design phases. Early collaboration leads to a more efficient design where systems such as electrical, HVAC, and plumbing are seamlessly integrated into the building's structure. This holistic approach avoids the need for last-minute design changes that often arise when MEPF systems are designed in isolation from the architecture.

Moreover, integrated design encourages **creative solutions** that enhance both aesthetics and function. For instance, MEPF engineers might develop custom solutions for air distribution that align with architectural features such as exposed ceilings or large windows. Similarly, architects can adjust their designs to accommodate MEPF systems in a way that does not compromise the building's aesthetic or spatial experience.

By recognizing the interdependence between architecture and MEPF systems, integrated design ensures that buildings are not only visually striking but also functional and efficient, creating a harmonious environment that benefits both users and the environment.

**Conclusion**

Understanding architectural design principles is vital to creating successful buildings that are both functional and beautiful. The relationship between form and function is key, as is the importance of space planning, aesthetics, and user experience. However, these considerations cannot be fully realized without recognizing the importance of integrating MEPF systems. By addressing these principles early in the design process, architects and MEPF engineers can collaborate to create smarter, more efficient, and more aesthetically pleasing buildings. Integrated design serves as the bridge between these two essential elements, ensuring that architectural vision and engineering expertise work together seamlessly.

# CHAPTER THREE

# Fundamentals of MEPF Systems

**Overview of MEPF Systems**

The integration of **Mechanical, Electrical, Plumbing, and Fire Protection (MEPF)** systems is integral to the function and operation of modern buildings. Each of these systems performs a vital role in maintaining a safe, comfortable, and efficient environment for occupants. When designed and coordinated properly, MEPF systems ensure a building operates efficiently while meeting the needs of its users. Understanding how each system functions and interacts with others is essential for architects, engineers, and construction professionals.

1. **Mechanical Systems (HVAC):**

   - **Heating, Ventilation, and Air Conditioning (HVAC)** systems are central to maintaining indoor comfort in buildings. These systems regulate temperature, humidity, and air quality, directly impacting occupant health, productivity, and well-being.
   - **Heating:** The heating component of HVAC systems ensures that spaces are warm during colder months. This can include central heating systems, radiant heating, or heat pumps, depending on the building's size and geographic location.
   - **Cooling:** Cooling systems, such as air conditioning or refrigeration, are essential for maintaining comfortable temperatures in warmer climates or during summer. These systems are designed to regulate indoor air temperature while removing excess moisture.
   - **Ventilation:** Proper ventilation ensures the supply of fresh air while expelling stale air from the building. Ventilation systems also filter

out pollutants, control humidity, and help maintain indoor air quality, which is especially important in spaces with high occupancy or specialized functions, such as healthcare facilities.

2. **Electrical Systems:**

   ◦ Electrical systems provide power to all aspects of a building, from lighting to equipment, and ensure the safe distribution of electricity throughout the structure.
   ◦ **Power Distribution**: Electrical systems consist of circuits, panels, transformers, and wiring that transport electrical energy from the power source to the building's electrical loads. The design of these systems needs to account for the electrical demand and ensure that circuits are properly sized to handle the building's needs.
   ◦ **Lighting**: Lighting systems serve both functional and aesthetic purposes. From general lighting to task-specific illumination, electrical engineers design lighting solutions that enhance the building's usability and aesthetic appeal. Additionally, energy-efficient lighting options, such as LEDs, contribute to sustainability goals by reducing energy consumption.
   ◦ **Backup Power**: For critical systems such as elevators, emergency lighting, and medical equipment, buildings require reliable backup power systems. These may include generators, uninterruptible power supplies (UPS), or battery-powered systems designed to ensure continuous operation during power failures.

3. **Plumbing Systems:**

   ◦ Plumbing systems manage the supply of water and the disposal of waste in a building. These systems consist of water supply, drainage, and venting mechanisms that must all be properly designed and integrated to maintain efficiency and hygiene.
   ◦ **Water Supply**: Plumbing systems bring potable water into the building for various uses, including drinking, washing, cooking, and sanitation. The design of the water supply system depends on factors such as pressure, demand, and the location of the water source.
   ◦ **Drainage and Waste Removal**: Drainage systems remove wastewater and sewage from the building, directing it to the municipal sewer

system or a septic tank. This system includes pipes, traps, and vents to ensure that waste is properly handled and that odors are eliminated.

- **Stormwater Management**: Plumbing systems must also handle stormwater runoff from roofs, paved surfaces, and landscaping. Stormwater management is essential in preventing flooding, erosion, and damage to the building's foundation and surrounding area.

4. **Fire Protection Systems:**

- Fire protection is a critical component of building safety and often integrates with other MEPF systems to create a safe environment for building occupants. Fire protection systems are designed to detect, contain, and extinguish fires, and they must comply with building codes and safety regulations.
- **Fire Detection**: Fire detection systems, such as smoke and heat detectors, are responsible for alerting occupants and emergency services in the event of a fire. These systems are often connected to the building's alarm system, which automatically activates in case of a fire.
- **Fire Suppression**: Fire suppression systems, including sprinklers, standpipes, and fire extinguishers, are essential for controlling or extinguishing fires. Automatic sprinkler systems are typically installed in areas where the risk of fire is higher, such as kitchens, electrical rooms, and storage areas.
- **Smoke Control**: Smoke control systems are designed to limit the movement of smoke throughout a building during a fire. These systems typically involve smoke dampers, ventilation, and pressurization strategies to guide smoke out of the building and create safe evacuation routes for occupants.
- **Fire Alarm and Evacuation**: Fire alarm systems, including manual pull stations and automatic sensors, trigger alarms to notify occupants and emergency responders about the fire. In addition, evacuation systems—such as emergency lighting, exit signs, and clear escape routes—are crucial to guide people to safety.

**How Each System Supports Building Operations**

The MEPF systems collectively support the day-to-day operations of a building by providing essential services that ensure safety, comfort, and sustainability. The interaction between these systems is complex, and their effective integration is necessary for the building's smooth operation.

1. **Supporting Comfort and Health:**

   - **Mechanical (HVAC)** systems regulate the indoor environment to ensure that building occupants are comfortable, whether by maintaining optimal temperatures or ensuring the proper exchange of indoor and outdoor air.

Mechanical systems primarily deal with HVAC (Heating, Ventilation, and Air Conditioning), which regulate indoor environmental quality.
Core Components:

- Air Handling Units (AHUs)
- Ductwork
- Chillers, Boilers
- Exhaust systems
- VRF/VRV units

Design Interactions:

- Ceiling heights must accommodate ducting and units
- Mechanical rooms need sufficient space and access
- HVAC loads influenced by fenestration, insulation, and space use

   - **Electrical systems** support the functionality of lighting, temperature control, and other essential systems like elevators or medical equipment in specific building types such as hospitals or laboratories.

Electrical systems power the building, ensure safety, and enable technology infrastructure.
Core Components:

- Main distribution boards (MDB)
- Sub-panels and circuiting

- Lighting systems
- Emergency and backup systems (generators, UPS)
- Low-voltage systems: data, fire alarms, security

Design Interactions:

- Power loads depend on space function (e.g., labs vs. offices)
- Lighting must align with design aesthetics
- Routing of conduits should be coordinated with structure and finishes

  - **Plumbing systems** ensure the availability of clean water and the efficient removal of wastewater. They also support hygiene, a critical factor in both residential and commercial buildings.

Plumbing systems handle water supply, drainage, and special fluids (e.g., fire suppression or medical gases).
Core Components:

- Water supply and distribution
- Drainage and venting systems
- Pumps and storage tanks
- Rainwater harvesting and greywater recycling

Design Interactions:

- Vertical shaft alignment through bathrooms/kitchens
- Drain slopes influence floor-to-ceiling heights
- Noise insulation required near living/sleeping areas

  - **Fire protection systems** contribute to occupant safety, protecting people and property in the event of a fire by providing early detection, suppression, and safe evacuation.

1. **Supporting Energy Efficiency:**

  - **Mechanical systems** contribute to energy efficiency by optimizing heating and cooling processes. For example, modern HVAC systems use programmable thermostats, variable refrigerant flow (VRF) systems, and high-efficiency air filtration to minimize energy consumption.

- **Electrical systems** help reduce energy waste through efficient lighting solutions, smart building controls, and energy monitoring. Additionally, integrating renewable energy sources such as solar panels or wind turbines into electrical systems can further reduce a building's environmental footprint.
- **Plumbing systems** can support energy efficiency by incorporating water-saving technologies such as low-flow fixtures and water heaters with higher energy efficiency ratings. Additionally, systems that recycle or reuse water reduce overall water consumption and the energy needed to pump and treat water.
- **Fire protection systems** impact energy efficiency indirectly by integrating with the building's overall safety and operational systems. Efficient fire suppression systems can reduce the need for excessive cooling after a fire or minimize damage to the building that might otherwise require costly repairs.

2. **Supporting Safety and Code Compliance:**

- **Mechanical systems** must comply with building codes that ensure proper ventilation, heating, and cooling for safe occupancy. In high-rise buildings, for example, HVAC systems must be designed to support smoke control and emergency evacuation strategies in the event of a fire.
- **Electrical systems** must adhere to local electrical codes to ensure safety in power distribution and lighting. These codes are designed to prevent electrical hazards, such as fires or shocks, and require rigorous testing and inspections.
- **Plumbing systems** must comply with codes that dictate safe water use, waste disposal, and the prevention of waterborne diseases. Proper backflow prevention, for instance, ensures that contaminated water does not re-enter the building's potable water supply.
- **Fire protection systems** are governed by strict codes, including NFPA (National Fire Protection Association) standards, that dictate where fire suppression and detection systems must be installed, how they should function, and when they must be tested. These systems must be regularly inspected and maintained to remain compliant.

## Challenges in Designing and Integrating MEPF Systems

Designing and integrating MEPF systems into a building involves several challenges that must be addressed during the design, construction, and operational phases.

1. **Space and Coordination Constraints**: MEPF systems require significant space for installation. Coordinating the layout of ducts, pipes, wiring, and fire protection systems within the building's structure can be complex, particularly in buildings with limited space or intricate architectural designs.

2. **System Compatibility and Coordination**: The proper coordination of MEPF systems is crucial to ensure they function optimally. For example, HVAC ductwork and electrical conduits must be routed in a way that doesn't interfere with plumbing systems. Additionally, fire protection systems must be integrated into the overall building design without compromising accessibility or aesthetics.

3. **Energy Efficiency and Sustainability**: The need for energy-efficient MEPF systems is increasing as building regulations become more stringent. Designers must balance the demand for comfort and safety with the need to minimize energy consumption and environmental impact. Integrating renewable energy sources and smart building technologies can provide solutions, but they may also require additional investment and planning.

4. **Maintenance and Flexibility**: MEPF systems must be designed with ease of maintenance in mind. As buildings evolve over time, systems need to be adaptable to future changes, whether they involve expanding the building or upgrading certain functions. For instance, electrical systems should allow for easy upgrades to support new equipment or higher power demands.

## Conclusion

The MEPF systems are crucial to ensuring that buildings operate effectively, efficiently, and safely. Their successful integration requires careful planning, design, and coordination to create a functional and comfortable environment for occupants. Understanding the fundamentals of these systems, including how they interact with one another and contribute to building performance, is essential for achieving a harmonious integrated design. As buildings continue to evolve, the role of MEPF systems in supporting sustainability, energy efficiency, and occupant safety will only grow in importance.

# CHAPTER FOUR

# Challenges in Traditional Design Approach

In the world of building design, traditional approaches to architectural and engineering design have long been prevalent. However, as the complexity of building systems increases, particularly with the growing emphasis on sustainability, energy efficiency, and occupant comfort, it has become clear that these traditional methods no longer meet the needs of modern buildings. Traditional approaches often involve siloed working methods, where different disciplines—architects, mechanical engineers, electrical engineers, and plumbing specialists—work independently, with little collaboration between them.

This chapter explores the key challenges of traditional building design approaches, the issues arising from siloed workflows, and how these challenges affect both the design process and the final building outcome.

**Siloed Working Methods**

One of the most significant issues in traditional design approaches is the siloed nature of work between various design disciplines. In the traditional method, architectural teams, MEPF engineers, and other consultants work separately, often focusing on their own areas without consulting one another until later in the design process. While this approach may have worked in the past, it presents several key challenges in today's complex building designs.

1. **Lack of Coordination**: In traditional design processes, architects and MEPF engineers typically work within their own boundaries. Architects are responsible for creating the building's overall design, space planning, and aesthetics, while MEPF engineers design the systems necessary for the building's operations, including heating, cooling, lighting, and

plumbing. These systems, while critical to a building's function, are often designed without a full understanding of the architectural elements and vice versa. As a result, the two sides may not align well, leading to significant coordination issues later in the process.

Problems With Siloed Workflows:

- Architectural drawings are finalized before MEPF coordination
- MEPF systems are forced to adapt to fixed spatial constraints
- Late-stage redesigns lead to cost overruns and delays

For example, the placement of HVAC ducts, plumbing pipes, fire sprinkler pipes or electrical wiring may conflict with the architectural layout. In traditional methods, these clashes often arise after construction has already begun, leading to costly rework and delays. In the worst-case scenario, systems might need to be completely redesigned to fit within the building's structure, further inflating costs and extending the construction timeline.

1. **Delayed Identification of Design Issues**: When architectural and MEPF designs are created in isolation, it often results in design issues being identified too late in the process. For instance, the architect may design a building with large open spaces, but the HVAC system may not have enough capacity to meet the ventilation and heating needs. Similarly, plumbing systems may run into space constraints, especially in tall or compact buildings, where the architect's design may not allow sufficient room for piping. These types of issues are typically only identified after design drawings are completed, which leads to costly and time-consuming changes.

Change is inevitable, but lack of version control or late communication exacerbates the impact.

Real-World Examples:

- Electrical conduits rerouted due to unnotified HVAC redesign
- Equipment resizing leading to structural and spatial redesign

Solutions:

- Shared project platforms (like BIM 360)
- Scheduled coordination reviews with all stakeholders

3. **Increased Costs**: Traditional siloed methods can contribute to significant cost overruns. This is primarily due to the need for rework, the duplication of efforts, and the extra time spent resolving conflicts between architectural and engineering designs. Additionally, when design issues are discovered late in the process, construction delays can result in additional costs, both in terms of labor and materials. Without early collaboration, teams may fail to identify cost-saving opportunities that could be easily implemented if all disciplines were working together from the start.

Projects with poor coordination often face:

- 15–30% increase in change orders
- 5–10% schedule delays
- Loss of client trust

4. **Inefficiency in Communication**: In a traditional workflow, architects and MEPF engineers typically operate on different timelines, leading to a lack of ongoing communication. Architects may complete a preliminary design without fully consulting the engineers, who then have to adjust systems based on the architectural plans they receive. This back-and-forth results in inefficient communication and a lack of timely feedback, ultimately slowing down the design process and affecting the overall project schedule.

Different teams use varied platforms, formats, and terminologies. This hinders effective collaboration.

- Architects use CAD/BIM for spatial layouts
- Engineers model systems in specialized software
- Contractors interpret 2D drawings without access to the latest 3D updates.

5. **Limited Innovation**: Traditional methods of design often restrict the creative potential of teams. With siloed work, architects and MEPF

engineers are less likely to collaborate on innovative solutions that could combine both aesthetics and functionality. For instance, innovative energy-efficient design concepts, such as passive heating or cooling strategies, may not be explored because MEPF systems are not factored into the building's layout early on. An integrated design approach, where all teams collaborate from the start, encourages the exploration of more creative, forward-thinking solutions that benefit both architecture and engineering.

Projects suffer from several recurring issues that stem from poor interdisciplinary collaboration:

- Clash detection failures: Ducts running through beams, lighting obstructed by piping
- Inadequate space allocation: Plant rooms undersized, insufficient shaft space
- Redundant work: Frequent design changes ripple through teams
- Delayed decision-making: Waiting on finalized architectural drawings slows MEPF design

**Clash Detection and Rework Issues**

One of the most significant issues with traditional building design methods is the lack of a structured approach to detecting clashes and resolving conflicts. In a siloed system, architects and engineers often submit their respective plans without fully considering the impact on one another's work. These clashes can take many forms, including:

1. **Space Conflicts**: A common clash occurs when mechanical systems such as ductwork or plumbing pipes interfere with architectural features. For example, the architect might design a ceiling height that does not accommodate the size of HVAC ducts, or a bathroom layout may block access to plumbing pipes. In a traditional approach, these issues are often discovered during construction, resulting in delays and additional costs as changes are made to the building structure to accommodate these systems.

2. **Structural Clashes**: MEPF systems often need to be installed within the building's structural framework. However, if architects and engineers do not collaborate closely, issues arise where plumbing or electrical systems

clash with beams, columns, or load-bearing walls. These clashes can severely impact the structural integrity of the building or require costly redesigns.

3. **System Interference**: Electrical systems can sometimes interfere with plumbing or mechanical systems. For example, electrical conduit may be routed through the same space as HVAC ductwork, leading to spatial conflicts. If these issues aren't detected early, they can result in considerable disruption during the construction phase.

The traditional approach to resolving these clashes usually involves rework—sometimes even significant portions of the building design need to be redone. This can lead to delays, additional costs, and even legal disputes if the building cannot be completed on time or within budget.

In many cases, the result is suboptimal performance from the building's systems, as the final design is often a compromise made to address these late-stage conflicts. However, with the advent of modern technologies like Building Information Modeling (BIM), many of these issues can be resolved earlier in the design phase, ensuring smoother and more efficient construction.

**Impact on Sustainability and Efficiency**

Sustainability and energy efficiency are critical considerations in modern building design, and traditional design methods often make it challenging to achieve optimal performance in these areas. Traditional siloed approaches are often too fragmented to design buildings that can meet rigorous sustainability standards. Without integrated collaboration, opportunities for energy-efficient solutions may be overlooked or poorly implemented.

1. **Energy Efficiency**: Traditional methods often fail to fully consider the energy needs of a building. For instance, an architect may design a building with large windows for natural light, but the MEPF systems may not be able to accommodate passive heating or cooling strategies to balance the additional heat load caused by solar gain. This oversight can lead to increased energy consumption and reduced performance.

2. **Sustainable Design**: Architects often focus on building aesthetics and layout without fully considering the sustainability of the MEPF systems. For example, designing a building with energy-efficient windows is a great step, but if the HVAC system is not properly designed to

complement this feature, it may render the energy-saving efforts ineffective. In an integrated design process, these concerns would be addressed early, ensuring that sustainable solutions are incorporated into every aspect of the design.

**Lack of Flexibility in Response to Changing Needs**

Another challenge with the traditional approach is that it tends to be inflexible in responding to changes in building needs. As projects progress, client requirements may change, new technologies may emerge, or building codes may be updated. In traditional design, changes to one part of the design often necessitate changes to multiple other systems, resulting in cascading redesigns.

For example, if the architect changes the building's layout after the MEPF systems have been designed, the engineers may need to redesign the plumbing, electrical, and HVAC systems to accommodate the new design. This process can be time-consuming and costly, and often leads to delays that push back the project timeline.

**Conclusion**

Traditional building design approaches, characterized by siloed work between architects, MEPF engineers, and other stakeholders, present significant challenges to the efficient and effective design of modern buildings. The lack of coordination, clash detection, and integration between disciplines results in higher costs, delays, and suboptimal performance. As buildings grow in complexity, these issues are increasingly difficult to overcome with traditional methods. The need for a more integrated design approach, where all disciplines collaborate from the outset, is clear. An integrated approach not only improves communication and coordination but also enhances the building's sustainability, energy efficiency, and overall performance.

Traditional workflows have inherent weaknesses that increase risk, cost, and dissatisfaction. In the following chapters, we will explore how BIM, integrated teams, and modern design management tools are transforming the way buildings are conceived and delivered.

Reflection Questions:

- Have past projects suffered from late-stage redesigns?
- What tools or habits could better support collaboration in your workflow?

# CHAPTER FIVE

# Benefits of Integrated MEPF Design

The integration of **Mechanical, Electrical, Plumbing, and Fire Protection (MEPF)** systems is essential for the successful design and operation of modern buildings. Traditionally, MEPF systems were designed in isolation by separate teams, often leading to inefficiencies, delays, and costly redesigns. In contrast, an integrated MEPF design approach ensures that all systems are designed and coordinated simultaneously, from the outset of the project. This collaborative approach provides several key benefits, not only in terms of technical performance but also with respect to energy efficiency, cost savings, sustainability, and occupant comfort.

In this chapter, we will explore the major advantages of an integrated MEPF design, focusing on **improved coordination, energy efficiency, cost-effectiveness**, and **enhanced system performance**.

**1. Improved Coordination and Collaboration**

One of the most significant benefits of integrated MEPF design is the improved coordination and collaboration between the various design disciplines—mechanical, electrical, plumbing, and fire protection engineers—alongside architects and other project stakeholders.

1. **Early Involvement of MEPF Engineers**: In an integrated approach, MEPF engineers are involved from the very beginning of the design process. This early involvement allows engineers to understand the architect's vision, including the spatial layout, structural design, and aesthetic considerations. By engaging with architects and other stakeholders, MEPF engineers can provide valuable input on the feasibility of designs, ensuring that the systems work seamlessly within the architectural and structural constraints.

2. **Streamlined Communication:** Integrated MEPF design fosters continuous communication between architects, engineers, and other stakeholders throughout the design process. This reduces the chances of miscommunication, ensuring that everyone is aligned with the project's goals. Real-time collaboration platforms, such as **Building Information Modeling (BIM)**, further enhance coordination, allowing for virtual visualization of the systems, identification of conflicts, and quicker resolution of potential issues.

3. **Reduced Design Conflicts:** In traditional siloed design processes, clashes between architectural elements and MEPF systems often emerge late in the design or construction phases. These clashes result in delays, costly revisions, and rework. With integrated design, conflicts are identified and addressed early, preventing last-minute adjustments. For example, if HVAC ducts interfere with a structural beam or if plumbing systems need to be rerouted, these issues can be resolved during the design phase, reducing costly delays during construction.

### 2. Enhanced Energy Efficiency

Energy efficiency is a key priority in modern building design, and integrated MEPF systems play a crucial role in achieving high-performance, energy-efficient buildings. The benefits of integrated design in terms of energy efficiency are evident across multiple systems, including heating, cooling, lighting, water supply, and waste management.

1. **Optimized HVAC and Building Envelope:** HVAC systems are typically the largest energy consumers in a building. An integrated design approach ensures that the HVAC system is designed in coordination with the building's envelope (i.e., walls, windows, insulation, and roof). Architects and MEPF engineers can collaborate to optimize the building's passive heating and cooling strategies, reducing the reliance on mechanical systems.

For example, architects can design facades with high-performance glazing that minimizes heat loss in winter and reduces solar gain in summer. MEPF engineers can then design HVAC systems that complement this energy-efficient envelope, ensuring that the systems are properly sized and designed for optimal performance.

1. **Energy-Efficient Lighting**: Electrical systems are another major source of energy consumption in buildings. Integrated MEPF design allows for the incorporation of **energy-efficient lighting** solutions such as **LED lighting**, **daylight harvesting**, and **occupancy sensors**. These technologies ensure that lighting is used only when necessary, reducing energy waste. Additionally, electrical engineers can design lighting systems that complement natural light, optimizing energy use during the day.

2. **Efficient Water Use**: Plumbing systems, when integrated into the overall building design, can significantly reduce water consumption. The use of **low-flow fixtures**, **water-efficient appliances**, and **rainwater harvesting systems**can help conserve water without compromising comfort or functionality. Integrated plumbing design ensures that these systems are installed correctly, with consideration for the building's specific needs and occupancy levels.

3. **Renewable Energy Integration**: Integrated MEPF design also facilitates the incorporation of **renewable energy sources**, such as **solar panels**, **wind turbines**, and **geothermal systems**. Architects and MEPF engineers can collaborate to determine the feasibility of renewable energy integration, optimizing system placement and design to maximize energy generation. For instance, solar panels can be integrated into the building's roof design, while geothermal systems can be incorporated into the HVAC system for heating and cooling.

By incorporating energy-efficient strategies into all aspects of the MEPF systems, integrated design helps buildings achieve lower energy consumption, reduced utility costs, and a smaller environmental footprint.

### 3. Cost-Effectiveness and Financial Benefits

Although the initial investment in an integrated MEPF design approach may be higher, the long-term financial benefits are substantial. Cost savings are achieved through optimized system design, reduced construction delays, and improved operational efficiency. Here are some of the key financial advantages of integrated MEPF design:

1. **Reduced Construction and Rework Costs**: In traditional siloed design approaches, design conflicts and system clashes often lead to costly rework, delays, and change orders. These issues can significantly increase the overall cost of the project. By resolving conflicts early in the

design process, integrated MEPF design reduces the need for rework and ensures a smoother construction process. This not only saves money but also reduces the risk of cost overruns and project delays.

2. **Optimized System Sizing**: Integrated design enables engineers to properly size the MEPF systems based on the building's actual requirements. For example, HVAC systems can be designed to meet the building's specific heating and cooling loads, avoiding the need for oversized systems that waste energy and cost more to install. Similarly, plumbing systems can be designed to meet the exact water demand of the building, ensuring that no unnecessary pipes or fixtures are installed.

3. **Long-Term Operational Savings**: The efficiency of integrated MEPF systems leads to significant savings over the life of the building. Energy-efficient HVAC systems, lighting, and water-saving fixtures reduce utility bills, while high-performance building envelopes minimize heating and cooling costs. Furthermore, integrated systems are easier to maintain and operate, reducing long-term maintenance and repair costs. These savings can offset the initial investment in integrated design and result in a more cost-effective building in the long run.

4. **Increased Building Value**: Integrated MEPF design not only improves the building's performance but also enhances its value in the market. Energy-efficient and sustainable buildings are increasingly sought after by tenants and buyers. Buildings that incorporate renewable energy systems and achieve certifications such as **LEED (Leadership in Energy and Environmental Design)** or **BREEAM (Building Research Establishment Environmental Assessment Method)** are more attractive to environmentally conscious occupants and investors. This can lead to higher rental rates, increased occupancy, and greater resale value.


### 4. Enhanced System Performance and Reliability

When MEPF systems are designed in isolation, they may not perform optimally, leading to inefficiencies, breakdowns, and poor user experience. Integrated MEPF design ensures that systems are harmonized, resulting in improved performance and reliability.

1. **Seamless System Integration**: Integrated MEPF design allows for seamless coordination between various systems, ensuring that they function together efficiently. For example, the HVAC system can be

designed to work in conjunction with the building's lighting and occupancy sensors, optimizing energy use based on the number of occupants in the space. Plumbing systems can be integrated with the building's waste management strategies to minimize water usage and ensure effective waste removal.

2. **Higher Comfort Levels**: An integrated approach to HVAC and lighting design results in a more comfortable environment for building occupants. For example, by using advanced HVAC systems that provide consistent temperature control and proper ventilation, integrated design ensures optimal comfort levels throughout the building. Similarly, energy-efficient lighting and natural light strategies reduce glare and enhance visual comfort, contributing to a better overall occupant experience.

3. **Improved Safety and Compliance**: Fire protection systems are a crucial component of MEPF design. Integrated fire protection design ensures that fire suppression systems, such as sprinklers, smoke detectors, and fire alarms, are properly coordinated with other building systems. This coordination ensures that the fire protection systems are fully operational, reducing the risk of false alarms and improving overall safety. Additionally, integrated fire protection systems help buildings comply with local building codes and safety regulations.

### Conclusion

The integration of MEPF systems within the building design process provides numerous advantages, ranging from improved coordination and collaboration to energy efficiency, cost savings, and enhanced system performance. By engaging all stakeholders early in the design process, integrated MEPF design ensures that building systems work together harmoniously, optimizing performance and reducing the risk of costly conflicts and redesigns. As buildings continue to grow in complexity and sustainability becomes increasingly important, integrated MEPF design offers a clear path to achieving high-performance, cost-effective, and comfortable buildings that meet the needs of both occupants and the environment.

# CHAPTER SIX

# Codes, Standards, and Compliance

In the design and construction of buildings, adherence to codes, standards, and regulations is crucial for ensuring the safety, sustainability, and functionality of the structure. These codes and standards govern everything from building design to the installation of **Mechanical, Electrical, Plumbing, and Fire Protection (MEPF)** systems, ensuring that all aspects of the building operate as intended while maintaining safety, energy efficiency, and environmental compliance.

This chapter explores the significance of building codes and standards, including their role in MEPF design. It discusses the essential national and international regulations governing building systems and the need for coordination between architectural and engineering teams to ensure compliance with these regulations. The chapter will also highlight the importance of **documentation and coordination** in achieving compliance and meeting building code requirements.

**1. Understanding Building Codes and Standards**

Building codes are a set of rules and regulations that govern the design, construction, and alteration of buildings. These codes are established by government authorities or recognized organizations to ensure that buildings are safe, accessible, and meet environmental and performance standards. Compliance with building codes is mandatory, and failure to meet these codes can result in penalties, delays, or even the rejection of building plans.

**Standards** refer to established specifications or guidelines that provide detailed criteria for materials, systems, and components used in construction. While building codes provide broad requirements, standards give more specific instructions on how to meet those requirements. Many standards are developed by professional organizations and regulatory bodies, such as the **American Society of Heating, Refrigerating, and Air-Conditioning Engineers (ASHRAE)** and the **National Fire Protection Association (NFPA)**.

Together, codes and standards serve as the framework for designing safe, efficient, and sustainable buildings. These regulations ensure that all building systems—especially MEPF systems—are designed and installed properly to meet health, safety, and environmental goals.

**2. Key Codes and Standards in MEPF Design**

In the realm of MEPF systems, there are several important codes and standards that guide the design, installation, and operation of mechanical, electrical, plumbing, and fire protection systems. Understanding these codes is essential to achieving compliance and ensuring that building systems are safe, energy-efficient, and function as intended.

1. **National Building Code (NBC):** The **National Building Code (NBC)** provides comprehensive guidelines for the design and construction of buildings. It covers all aspects of building safety, including structural integrity, accessibility, fire safety, and mechanical, electrical, and plumbing systems. The NBC is widely adopted in various countries and often forms the foundation for local building regulations.

   In terms of MEPF systems, the NBC establishes specific requirements for the design, installation, and maintenance of mechanical, electrical, and plumbing systems, ensuring they meet safety, performance, and environmental standards.

1. **ASHRAE Standards:** The **American Society of Heating, Refrigerating, and Air-Conditioning Engineers (ASHRAE)** is one of the leading organizations in the field of HVAC design. ASHRAE provides a series of standards and guidelines for HVAC systems, including requirements for energy efficiency, ventilation, and indoor air quality.

   ○ **ASHRAE 90.1:** The **Energy Standard for Buildings** (ASHRAE 90.1) sets requirements for the energy efficiency of buildings, including standards for HVAC systems, lighting, and the building envelope. This standard is particularly important for achieving energy-efficient buildings that meet environmental and sustainability goals.

- ◦ **ASHRAE 62.1**: The **Ventilation for Acceptable Indoor Air Quality** standard (ASHRAE 62.1) provides requirements for the ventilation systems in buildings, ensuring that indoor air quality meets the needs of building occupants.

2. **National Electrical Code (NEC)**: The **National Electrical Code (NEC)** provides a comprehensive set of rules and guidelines for electrical installations. It governs the design, installation, and inspection of electrical systems, including wiring, outlets, lighting, and safety features such as grounding, overcurrent protection, and emergency power systems.

Compliance with the NEC is essential to ensuring the safety and reliability of electrical systems in buildings. Electrical engineers must adhere to the code to prevent electrical hazards such as fires, electrocution, and system malfunctions.

4. **Plumbing Codes (International Plumbing Code – IPC)**: Plumbing systems are governed by plumbing codes, such as the **International Plumbing Code (IPC)** and the **Uniform Plumbing Code (UPC)**. These codes set standards for the design, installation, and maintenance of water supply, drainage, waste disposal, and stormwater systems.

   - ◦ **IPC** provides requirements for the sizing and installation of pipes, fixtures, and appliances, ensuring that plumbing systems meet health and safety standards.
   - ◦ **Water Efficiency**: Plumbing codes also include guidelines for water conservation, such as the installation of water-saving fixtures (low-flow toilets, faucets) and systems for recycling greywater.

5. **Fire Protection Codes (NFPA)**: The **National Fire Protection Association (NFPA)** develops standards for fire protection systems. These standards ensure that buildings are equipped with the necessary systems to detect, suppress, and manage fires. Fire protection codes are critical to ensuring the safety of building occupants.

   - ◦ **NFPA 13**: This standard covers the design and installation of **sprinkler systems**, specifying the type of systems required in different areas of the building based on occupancy and risk factors.

- ○ **NFPA 72**: This standard governs the design and installation of **fire alarm systems**, ensuring that buildings are equipped with adequate detection and notification devices to alert occupants in the event of a fire.
- ○ **NFPA 101**: The **Life Safety Code** (NFPA 101) provides requirements for building egress, fire-resistant materials, and fire-rated assemblies, all of which play a role in maintaining safe evacuation routes and protecting occupants during a fire.

6. **Local Codes and Regulations**: In addition to national and international standards, local building codes and regulations must also be considered. These regulations often address specific regional conditions, such as seismic requirements in earthquake-prone areas or hurricane-resistant designs in coastal regions. Local codes ensure that buildings are designed to withstand environmental challenges and meet the specific needs of the community.

### 3. Compliance and Coordination in MEPF Design

Compliance with codes and standards is not only necessary for safety and functionality but is also legally required. Inadequate compliance can result in fines, delays, and the inability to occupy the building. As a result, coordination between architects, engineers, and contractors is critical to ensuring that all aspects of the MEPF design meet the relevant regulations.

1. **Coordinating MEPF Systems**: Ensuring that mechanical, electrical, plumbing, and fire protection systems are coordinated and comply with codes requires early and continuous collaboration between the respective teams. In an integrated design approach, the MEPF engineers work alongside the architects and structural engineers to design systems that align with building codes and performance standards while meeting the project's goals.

2. **Documentation and Approvals**: Proper documentation is essential for ensuring compliance with building codes. Detailed drawings, specifications, and calculations must be submitted to regulatory authorities for approval. MEPF engineers need to provide documentation that demonstrates how the systems meet code requirements, including system capacities, energy efficiency measures,

and safety features. For example, fire protection systems must be approved by local fire departments to ensure they meet the necessary safety standards.

3. **Inspection and Testing**: During construction, building systems are typically subject to inspection by local authorities or third-party agencies to ensure compliance with the applicable codes. MEPF systems, such as HVAC, electrical, plumbing, and fire protection systems, must be tested to verify that they operate correctly and meet performance standards. After installation, final commissioning ensures that the systems function as designed.

4. **Code Updates and Ongoing Compliance**: Codes and standards are regularly updated to reflect advances in technology, changes in safety requirements, and environmental goals. Architects and MEPF engineers must stay informed about updates to local and international building codes to ensure that the systems they design continue to meet current standards. Ongoing compliance is essential not only during the design and construction phases but throughout the building's lifecycle, including regular inspections and maintenance of MEPF systems.

### 4. The Role of Technology in Ensuring Compliance

Modern technologies like **Building Information Modelling (BIM)**, energy simulation software, and smart sensors have revolutionized the way compliance is ensured in building design. These technologies provide tools to model, simulate, and analyse building systems to verify that they meet relevant codes and standards.

1. **BIM for Code Compliance**: BIM enables architects and engineers to design and visualize building systems in a 3D environment, making it easier to identify potential conflicts and ensure that all systems meet code requirements. BIM models can be programmed to check that systems are compliant with local regulations, reducing the risk of errors and conflicts during construction.

2. **Energy Modelling and Simulations**: Energy modelling tools allow engineers to simulate the performance of HVAC, lighting, and plumbing systems under various conditions. These simulations can verify that systems meet energy efficiency standards and are in compliance with codes like ASHRAE 90.1.

3. **Smart Building Technologies**: Advanced sensors and automation systems in smart buildings ensure ongoing compliance with building codes. For example, sensors can monitor air quality and adjust ventilation based on occupancy or environmental conditions. Fire detection and suppression systems can automatically activate in the event of a fire, ensuring the building remains compliant with fire safety regulations.

## Conclusion

Adhering to building codes, standards, and regulations is fundamental to ensuring the safety, performance, and functionality of a building. In the design of MEPF systems, compliance is crucial not only to meet legal requirements but also to create safe, efficient, and sustainable buildings. An integrated approach to design, where architects and MEPF engineers work together from the outset, facilitates the coordination and compliance necessary to meet these standards. By using advanced technologies and maintaining clear communication and documentation, design teams can ensure that their projects comply with the latest codes, providing a foundation for a successful and compliant building.

# CHAPTER SEVEN

# Early Stage Collaboration is the key

The success of a building project—whether residential, commercial, or institutional—often hinges on the collaborative efforts of all design and construction stakeholders, particularly at the early stages. Traditionally, design processes have followed a linear progression where different teams—architects, MEPF engineers, structural engineers, and contractors—work within their own silos, each contributing their piece of the puzzle in isolation. However, as buildings have grown more complex, it has become increasingly evident that an integrated approach, beginning with early-stage collaboration, is critical to creating efficient, sustainable, and high-performing buildings.

Early collaboration fosters better communication, reduces mistakes and rework, enhances system coordination, and ultimately leads to more successful outcomes. This chapter will explore the importance of early-stage collaboration, highlighting key strategies, benefits, and methods for integrating **Mechanical, Electrical, Plumbing, and Fire Protection (MEPF)** engineers with architects and other stakeholders from the very beginning of the design process.

**1. The Importance of Early Collaboration in Building Design**

Early collaboration between architects, MEPF engineers, and other stakeholders is a key component of integrated design. The earlier these professionals can work together, the more likely it is that the building design will meet both functional and aesthetic goals, while also being efficient and sustainable. Collaboration in the early stages of a project ensures that all design elements are considered in relation to one another and that potential conflicts or issues are identified and addressed before construction begins.

1. **Creating a Unified Vision**: When all key players are involved early on, they can align their goals and visions for the project. This leads to a more cohesive design where the architect's vision for the building's form and function is complemented by the MEPF systems and other technical components. For instance, MEPF engineers can help ensure that the HVAC system is sized appropriately for the building's design, and architects can modify the building's layout to accommodate these systems without compromising on aesthetic goals.

This alignment is crucial for the successful implementation of energy-efficient and sustainable design strategies. Architects may propose natural lighting or ventilation solutions, and MEPF engineers can work to integrate these into the HVAC or electrical systems, optimizing both the environmental and functional performance of the building.

1. **Addressing Problems Early**: One of the greatest advantages of early-stage collaboration is the ability to identify and resolve problems before they escalate into costly issues during construction. For example, conflicts between structural elements, MEPF systems, and architectural features can be addressed at the design stage, preventing delays and rework later on. Early collaboration allows teams to discuss potential challenges and explore creative solutions, avoiding the pitfalls of designing in isolation.

For example, MEPF systems such as ductwork, piping, and electrical wiring require careful coordination with structural and architectural elements. If the architect designs a ceiling with a specific aesthetic goal, MEPF engineers can advise on the space required for ducts and pipes, ensuring that these systems can be accommodated without interfering with the design. Similarly, architects can adjust their designs based on the recommendations of MEPF engineers, creating a seamless integration of all building systems.

3. **Incorporating Sustainable Strategies**: Sustainable design is increasingly becoming a priority in modern building projects, and early collaboration plays a crucial role in achieving sustainability goals. From the beginning of the project, architects and MEPF engineers can work together to incorporate energy-efficient systems, renewable energy sources, and

sustainable materials into the building design. Early coordination ensures that the building's energy performance is optimized, and that systems like HVAC, lighting, plumbing, and waste management align with the project's sustainability targets.

For example, architects might design a building to maximize natural light, and MEPF engineers can collaborate to integrate passive solar heating or daylight-responsive lighting systems. Similarly, early-stage discussions can focus on water conservation strategies, such as low-flow fixtures or rainwater harvesting systems, which MEPF engineers can incorporate into their designs.

4. **Optimizing Cost Efficiency**: Early collaboration helps to identify cost-effective solutions from the outset. When all team members collaborate early, the design can be optimized for both performance and cost. The MEPF systems can be sized appropriately for the building's needs, reducing the likelihood of over-sizing, which leads to unnecessary equipment costs and energy consumption. Similarly, early-stage collaboration helps avoid expensive design changes and rework during the construction phase, saving both time and money.

For example, architects and engineers can collaborate on the layout of the building to ensure that mechanical systems like air conditioning or plumbing do not require excessive ductwork or piping. By optimizing the placement and size of these systems early in the design process, unnecessary costs can be avoided.

**2. Strategies for Effective Early Collaboration**

Effective early collaboration requires proactive communication, a shared understanding of the project goals, and the use of tools and processes that promote coordination. The following strategies are essential for ensuring a successful collaboration between architects, MEPF engineers, and other stakeholders:

1. **Design Charrettes: Design charrettes** are collaborative workshops where key project stakeholders—architects, engineers, contractors, and even clients—come together to discuss and brainstorm design concepts, address potential issues, and align on project goals. Charrettes typically take place early in the project and provide a platform for all team

members to contribute their expertise and ideas.

These workshops can be instrumental in fostering innovation and ensuring that all team members understand each other's perspectives. For example, MEPF engineers can explain the technical constraints of certain systems, while architects can present their design vision, and both groups can work together to find solutions that balance aesthetics, performance, and budget.

2. **Building Information Modelling (BIM): Building Information Modelling (BIM)** is a powerful tool that enhances early collaboration by allowing all project stakeholders to work in a shared digital environment. BIM enables architects, engineers, and contractors to create detailed 3D models of the building, which include not just architectural elements but also MEPF systems, structural components, and other building systems.

   The use of BIM allows for real-time collaboration, where team members can view, modify, and update the design as the project evolves. BIM also helps in detecting clashes or conflicts between different systems, such as HVAC ductwork conflicting with plumbing pipes or structural beams. Early identification of these issues allows for prompt resolution, reducing the likelihood of costly changes during construction.

3. **Interdisciplinary Meetings**: Regular interdisciplinary meetings between architects, MEPF engineers, and other stakeholders are essential for maintaining communication throughout the design process. These meetings should be scheduled regularly, particularly during the early stages of the project, to ensure that everyone is on the same page and to address any challenges that may arise.

   During these meetings, team members can share updates on their progress, raise any concerns, and collaborate on potential solutions. The meetings also allow for feedback from all disciplines, which ensures that the building systems work harmoniously and that the overall design is both functional and feasible.

4. **Early Site Visits and Contextual Analysis**: Early collaboration should also include site visits, where architects, engineers, and other

stakeholders can observe the physical site and its surrounding context. Understanding the site conditions—such as topography, climate, infrastructure, and access to resources—can have a significant impact on the design process.

For example, early site visits allow engineers to assess the feasibility of certain MEPF systems, such as plumbing connections to the municipal water supply or the location of electrical substations. This site-specific analysis ensures that the systems are designed to accommodate the site conditions and are feasible to install.

### 3. Benefits of Early Collaboration

The benefits of early-stage collaboration are wide-ranging and impact various aspects of the building project, including **design quality**, **project schedule**, **cost control**, and **overall performance**.

1. **Higher Design Quality**: Early collaboration leads to better-designed buildings that meet both aesthetic and functional goals. By considering MEPF systems from the outset, architects and engineers can create more cohesive and efficient designs that balance form, function, and technical performance. Integrated design often results in innovative solutions that might not have been considered in a traditional, siloed approach.

2. **Reduced Project Delays**: Early-stage collaboration helps to identify potential issues early in the design process, preventing delays later on. By addressing conflicts, optimizing systems, and ensuring that all team members are aligned, the likelihood of unexpected problems during construction is reduced. This leads to a smoother and faster construction process, allowing the building to be completed on time.

3. **Cost Savings**: The early identification of potential issues and the optimization of MEPF systems during the design phase help reduce costs. By preventing conflicts and rework during construction, early collaboration leads to fewer change orders, fewer delays, and better control of the project budget. Additionally, systems can be designed to be energy-efficient and cost-effective, leading to reduced operational costs over the life of the building.

4. **Improved Sustainability**: Collaborative design promotes the integration of sustainable practices from the very beginning. Architects and MEPF engineers can jointly explore energy-efficient strategies, renewable energy options, and water-saving technologies. This early focus on

sustainability ensures that the building meets or exceeds environmental standards, such as **LEED** or **BREEAM** certifications.

5. **Enhanced Occupant Comfort**: The early collaboration between architects and MEPF engineers ensures that building systems are designed to meet the needs of the occupants. HVAC systems, lighting, plumbing, and fire protection systems can be tailored to provide optimal comfort, safety, and convenience for building users. By considering these factors from the outset, the design process ensures that the final building is comfortable and functional.

**Conclusion**

Early-stage collaboration is the cornerstone of integrated building design, ensuring that all design disciplines—particularly architecture and MEPF systems—work together from the very beginning. By fostering communication, optimizing system coordination, and addressing potential conflicts early, this collaborative approach enhances the quality, efficiency, and sustainability of the final building. Through strategies such as design charrettes, BIM, interdisciplinary meetings, and site visits, architects and engineers can create a unified vision for the project that meets both functional and aesthetic goals while adhering to sustainability and performance standards.

# CHAPTER EIGHT

# Building Information Modelling (BIM)

Building Information Modelling (BIM) has revolutionized the design, construction, and operation of buildings. BIM is a digital tool that allows architects, engineers, contractors, and other stakeholders to collaboratively plan, design, construct, and manage a building through a shared, 3D virtual model. In this chapter, we will explore the role of BIM in the integrated design process, specifically how it enhances collaboration, streamlines workflows, aids in clash detection, and facilitates simulations for performance and energy efficiency.

The use of BIM in **Mechanical, Electrical, Plumbing, and Fire Protection (MEPF)** systems has become increasingly important for creating high-performance buildings. Through the creation of a comprehensive and data-rich 3D model, BIM helps integrate MEPF systems with architectural and structural designs, ensuring better coordination, more efficient system design, and ultimately, a more sustainable and cost-effective building.

### 1. The Role of BIM in Coordination and Collaboration

BIM is a collaborative platform that allows various project stakeholders, including architects, MEPF engineers, structural engineers, and contractors, to work together in real-time within a shared digital environment. This shared platform improves communication and helps integrate all design elements—architectural, structural, and MEPF systems—into a single, unified model.

1. **Collaboration Across Disciplines**: Traditionally, architects, engineers, and contractors worked in isolation, with each team designing their portion of the project independently. This siloed approach led to a lack of communication, design conflicts, and inefficiencies. In contrast, BIM

allows all stakeholders to view and interact with the same 3D model, creating a common language for communication. With BIM, architects can understand how MEPF systems interact with their designs, while MEPF engineers can see how their systems affect the building's overall architecture.

For instance, an architect can design a building's layout and plan spaces, while the MEPF engineers can immediately begin designing the HVAC, electrical, and plumbing systems within the same model. The ability to view changes in real time enables better decision-making and reduces the chances of conflicts that might arise later in the project.

1. **Real-Time Updates**: One of the most powerful features of BIM is its ability to facilitate real-time updates. As any member of the project team makes a change, the model automatically updates across all disciplines, ensuring that everyone is working with the most current version of the design. This dynamic interaction reduces the risk of discrepancies between different aspects of the design and helps prevent costly delays and errors.

## 2. BIM for Clash Detection and Problem Resolution

One of the most significant challenges in traditional building design is ensuring that the various systems do not interfere with one another. Conflicts or "clashes" between architectural, structural, and MEPF systems often go undetected until the construction phase, leading to costly rework, delays, and inefficiencies.

BIM helps address this challenge by enabling **clash detection**, a process in which the 3D model is analyzed to identify any potential conflicts between the building's systems before construction begins. Here's how BIM aids in clash detection and problem resolution:

1. **Identifying Conflicts Early**: By overlaying MEPF systems (e.g., ducts, pipes, electrical conduits) with architectural and structural components in the BIM model, the software automatically detects clashes between systems. For example, a large duct might clash with a structural beam or plumbing pipes might interfere with electrical conduits. In a traditional design process, such clashes might only be discovered during construction, causing delays and rework. With BIM, these conflicts can

be identified early in the design phase, allowing engineers and architects to collaborate and find solutions before construction starts.

2. **Streamlined Problem Solving**: Clash detection in BIM allows the project team to resolve conflicts virtually. For example, if an HVAC duct clashes with a structural beam, the design team can discuss alternatives, such as rerouting the duct, adjusting the beam's placement, or redesigning other systems to accommodate the clash. This proactive approach not only saves time and money but also ensures that systems are designed in a way that minimizes interference and optimizes space usage.

3. **Reduced Rework and Construction Delays**: Detecting and resolving clashes early in the design phase helps minimize rework and delays during construction. The use of BIM helps ensure that all systems fit together seamlessly, and the construction team can begin their work with greater confidence in the design. This reduces the likelihood of mistakes or changes that can derail a project timeline, ultimately saving both time and money.

### 3. BIM for Performance Simulations and Energy Modelling

In addition to improving coordination and detecting clashes, BIM can also be used to simulate building performance, including energy usage, airflow, lighting, and environmental impact. These simulations help designers optimize MEPF systems for energy efficiency and ensure that the building meets performance goals, such as sustainability and occupant comfort.

1. **Energy Efficiency Analysis**: BIM can integrate energy modelling tools that simulate how a building will consume energy throughout its life cycle. These models can help architects and MEPF engineers design systems that reduce energy consumption while maintaining comfort. For example, BIM can simulate the building's heating and cooling loads based on the building's geometry, orientation, and insulation. It can then suggest optimized HVAC systems to meet these needs without overdesigning.

This allows for more efficient designs that reduce operating costs and the building's environmental footprint. By modelling different HVAC systems, lighting strategies, and materials, BIM helps identify energy-saving solutions that may not be immediately apparent through traditional design methods.

2. **Lighting Simulation**: BIM allows designers to simulate lighting performance, including natural light, artificial light, and lighting distribution throughout the building. Using BIM, architects and electrical engineers can determine the optimal placement of windows, light fixtures, and shading devices to minimize energy consumption while ensuring adequate lighting levels for the building's occupants. Lighting simulations can also help achieve sustainable building certification, such as LEED or BREEAM, by optimizing lighting and reducing energy waste.

3. **Daylighting and Solar Gain Analysis**: BIM also enables **daylighting analysis**, which simulates how natural light enters the building at different times of the day and year. This can help optimize the use of natural light, reducing the need for artificial lighting and improving energy efficiency. Additionally, BIM can simulate **solar gain** to evaluate how solar radiation impacts the building's energy load and inform decisions about window placement, shading devices, or solar energy systems.

4. **Water Efficiency Modelling**: Plumbing systems can also be modelled within BIM to simulate water use and determine the best approach for water conservation. For instance, BIM can analyse water demand in different areas of the building and optimize the design of plumbing systems to meet these needs efficiently. It can also model rainwater harvesting systems, water treatment solutions, and stormwater management strategies to ensure that the building minimizes its environmental impact.

### 4. BIM for Facility Management and Maintenance

The use of BIM does not stop after construction. BIM can also be a powerful tool for the operation and maintenance of buildings throughout their lifecycle. The data-rich 3D model can be used by facility managers to track and manage building systems, ensuring that MEPF systems operate efficiently and remain in good condition over time.

1. **Asset Management**: Facility managers can use BIM to track the condition and performance of building systems, such as HVAC, electrical, plumbing, and fire protection systems. The model contains detailed data on each system's components, including manufacturer

information, maintenance schedules, and warranty details. This helps facility managers perform preventive maintenance and schedule repairs before issues arise, minimizing downtime and maximizing system performance.

2. **System Monitoring and Performance**: With the integration of **smart building technologies** and sensors, BIM can be used to monitor real-time system performance. For instance, HVAC systems can be equipped with sensors that track temperature, humidity, and airflow, providing data that can be analysed through BIM. This real-time data helps identify inefficiencies or performance issues, allowing for immediate corrective actions.

3. **Renovations and Upgrades**: As buildings age or their use changes over time, BIM models provide a valuable resource for planning renovations or system upgrades. Facility managers can use the BIM model to assess the existing systems and plan for future changes, such as retrofitting the building with more energy-efficient systems or adding new MEPF systems to accommodate changes in the building's use.

### 5. BIM for Sustainable Design and Certifications

BIM is an invaluable tool for achieving sustainability and securing green building certifications, such as **LEED**(Leadership in Energy and Environmental Design), **BREEAM** (Building Research Establishment Environmental Assessment Method), or **WELL Building Standard**. These certifications require rigorous performance standards for energy, water, air quality, and other factors, and BIM plays a central role in meeting these goals.

1. **Energy Modelling for LEED Certification**: BIM is often used to perform energy modelling and simulations required for LEED certification. For example, BIM can model energy consumption, carbon emissions, water usage, and waste management systems to ensure that the building meets the necessary sustainability criteria for various LEED credits.

2. **Water and Waste Reduction**: BIM can also assist in designing water-efficient systems, such as low-flow fixtures, rainwater harvesting systems, and greywater reuse. These systems contribute to LEED points related to water efficiency and help the building meet sustainability standards.

3. **Optimization of Building Systems**: BIM's ability to simulate and analyse the performance of building systems allows for the optimization of energy usage, which is a key factor in achieving green building certifications. By modelling and analysing different system configurations, BIM helps designers choose the most efficient systems, which can result in significant energy and cost savings.

## Conclusion

Building Information Modelling (BIM) has transformed the way buildings are designed, constructed, and operated. By providing a shared, data-rich 3D model, BIM enhances coordination, reduces clashes, and enables early-stage problem-solving, all of which lead to more efficient and cost-effective projects. BIM also supports performance simulations, energy modelling, and sustainable design, ensuring that buildings meet energy efficiency goals and adhere to sustainability standards. Furthermore, BIM continues to be valuable throughout the lifecycle of the building, aiding in facility management, maintenance, and system monitoring.

As BIM becomes more advanced and widely adopted, its role in the integrated design process will continue to grow, making it an indispensable tool for modern architecture, engineering, and construction.

# CHAPTER NINE

# Design Workflows and Coordination Tools

In the modern building design and construction industry, ensuring seamless coordination between various design disciplines is paramount to achieving a functional, efficient, and high-performing building. A major challenge faced by architecture, engineering, and construction (AEC) teams is managing complex workflows and ensuring that every team, from architects to MEPF engineers to contractors, is working from the same page. Without a streamlined workflow, communication breakdowns, errors, and inefficiencies can occur, leading to increased costs, delays, and suboptimal design outcomes.

The advancement of **design workflows and coordination tools** has revolutionized the way teams collaborate on building projects. Tools such as **Revit**, **Navisworks**, **AutoCAD MEPF**, and **real-time collaboration platforms** have transformed the industry by enabling multi-disciplinary coordination in a single digital environment. This chapter explores how these tools facilitate better communication, enhance coordination, and optimize project workflows, ultimately contributing to the success of the building design process.

**1. The Evolution of Design Workflows**

In traditional design workflows, each discipline typically operated in its own isolated environment. Architects, engineers, and contractors would work independently, often handing off documents or drawings between teams. This siloed approach led to problems such as poor coordination, late-stage design changes, conflicts between systems, and redundant or duplicated work. With such a process, miscommunications were common, leading to issues like poorly coordinated MEPF systems, inefficient use of space, and costly revisions during construction.

In contrast, modern design workflows prioritize collaboration from the very beginning. The advent of digital tools like **Building Information Modelling (BIM)** and **Cloud-based platforms** has redefined these workflows, enabling a more integrated, streamlined process. These tools have made it possible for architects, MEPF engineers, structural engineers, and contractors to all work from the same set of data and models in real-time.

1. **BIM as the Core of Modern Design Workflows: BIM** is at the heart of modern design workflows. It allows for the creation of a detailed, digital 3D model that contains not just the architectural design but also the mechanical, electrical, plumbing, and fire protection systems. This integrated model is used by all project stakeholders to coordinate, communicate, and review the design in a way that is far more efficient and effective than traditional workflows.

BIM makes it possible for all project members to visualize the design in three dimensions, rather than working with two-dimensional blueprints and paper-based communication. By using BIM, teams can make real-time changes, perform clash detection, and ensure all components of the building fit together correctly before construction begins.

The use of BIM also supports **data management**, where designers input data into the model, which can be tracked and analysed. This data includes everything from material specifications to maintenance schedules, creating a comprehensive resource that supports both design and operations.

1. **From Design to Construction**: Modern design workflows are not confined to the design phase alone; they extend all the way to construction and operation. **Integrated project delivery (IPD)** is a methodology that aligns with BIM and encourages collaborative working throughout the entire lifecycle of a project. IPD relies on integrated digital tools and early involvement from all key stakeholders to ensure efficient design, construction, and operation of the building.

## 2. Key Coordination Tools for the Integrated Design Process

Several design and coordination tools have become essential in facilitating the collaborative workflows of modern building projects. These tools allow different disciplines to work in harmony, enabling real-time collaboration and reducing the likelihood of errors. Let's explore some of the most widely used tools:

1. **Revit**: Revit is a powerful BIM tool primarily used by architects and MEPF engineers to create and manage building models. Revit is particularly suited for collaborative workflows because it allows all disciplines to work on the same file, updating the design in real-time. Changes made by one team member are automatically reflected in the model, ensuring that everyone is working from the most up-to-date information.

   - **Architectural Design**: Revit provides architects with a comprehensive suite of tools for modelling, visualizing, and documenting building designs. The software includes everything from space planning and design to detailed documentation and construction drawings.
   - **MEPF Design**: Revit also offers specialized tools for MEPF design, allowing engineers to model HVAC, electrical, and plumbing systems in 3D. It provides tools for sizing, placement, and optimization of these systems while ensuring they work within the building's structure and layout.
   - **Collaboration**: Revit's collaboration capabilities are enhanced through **Revit Server** or **Cloud Collaboration**, allowing team members to access and work on the model from any location. It supports real-time updates, ensuring that changes are immediately reflected in the shared model.

2. **Navisworks**: **Navisworks** is another essential coordination tool, primarily used for clash detection and review. Unlike Revit, which is a design tool, Navisworks is a review software that brings together data from different models (architectural, structural, MEPF) into a single platform. This helps ensure that all the systems work together and are free of conflicts.

   - **Clash Detection**: One of the primary functions of Navisworks is clash detection, which allows teams to detect conflicts between architectural, structural, and MEPF systems. For instance, if an HVAC duct clashes with a structural beam or electrical conduit, Navisworks will identify the issue, allowing teams to resolve it before construction begins.

- **4D and 5D Simulation**: Navisworks also supports **4D** (time) and **5D** (cost) simulation. This feature enables project teams to visualize the construction process in relation to the project timeline, allowing them to anticipate scheduling conflicts and manage resources more efficiently. It can also be used to track costs in real-time, which helps ensure the project stays within budget.

3. **AutoCAD MEPF: AutoCAD MEPF** is a specialized version of AutoCAD that focuses on the design of MEPF systems. It allows engineers to create 2D and 3D models of mechanical, electrical, and plumbing systems, ensuring they fit seamlessly within the architectural design. It also enables engineers to perform system analysis and make real-time adjustments to optimize system performance.

- **System-Specific Features**: AutoCAD MEPF includes specialized tools for designing HVAC systems, electrical distribution, fire protection systems, and plumbing layouts. The toolset allows engineers to create and modify detailed drawings while ensuring accuracy and compliance with building codes.
- **Coordination with Other Systems**: As part of the design workflow, AutoCAD MEPF allows easy integration with Revit, allowing MEPF models to be brought into the overall BIM model. This ensures that all disciplines are working with a unified model, reducing errors and improving coordination.

4. **Cloud-Based Collaboration Platforms: Cloud-based collaboration tools** have become essential in the modern design process, especially for teams working remotely or across multiple locations. These platforms allow all stakeholders to access and work on the building model in real-time, enabling faster decision-making and reducing communication delays.

- **Project Management**: Platforms like **Procore, Builder trend**, and **Aconex** provide comprehensive project management tools that allow teams to share documents, track progress, and communicate in real-time. These tools improve transparency, streamline communication, and ensure that everyone is aligned with the project's goals.

- **File Sharing and Version Control**: Cloud-based platforms ensure that all project files are stored in a central location, making it easier for teams to access and review up-to-date files. Version control features ensure that previous versions are preserved, so any changes can be traced and reverted if necessary.

5. **Integrated Design and Construction Platforms**: Some platforms integrate BIM, project management, scheduling, and cost tracking in a unified system. These platforms enable real-time collaboration, where team members can track progress, identify issues, and make decisions quickly. For example, platforms like **BIM 360** by Autodesk combine project documentation, coordination, clash detection, and model viewing into a single interface.

- **BIM 360**: This cloud-based platform helps project teams stay connected throughout the lifecycle of the building. It offers features for document management, design collaboration, issue tracking, and project coordination, streamlining the workflow from design through construction and handover.

## 3. Benefits of Integrated Design Workflows and Coordination Tools

1. **Improved Communication**: The use of coordinated tools like BIM, Navisworks, and cloud platforms fosters better communication across all project stakeholders. Real-time updates and shared digital models ensure that everyone is working from the same set of information, reducing the chances of miscommunication and errors. The result is a more efficient design process where every team member can collaborate effectively.

2. **Faster Decision-Making**: By having all relevant data in a centralized location, project teams can make faster, more informed decisions. For example, when issues arise during the design phase, stakeholders can quickly access the model, evaluate the impact, and suggest solutions. This speeds up the decision-making process, reducing delays and keeping the project on track.

3. **Better Coordination**: Coordination tools like BIM and Navisworks allow for early detection of design conflicts between different systems, such as HVAC ductwork, plumbing pipes, and structural elements. This reduces

the need for costly and time-consuming rework during construction. The ability to resolve issues digitally before construction begins results in a more streamlined, efficient project.

4. **Cost Savings**: By improving coordination, reducing rework, and optimizing system designs, integrated design workflows lead to significant cost savings. Early collaboration ensures that designs are efficient, systems are sized correctly, and potential issues are identified before construction starts. This minimizes unnecessary costs and helps the project stay within budget.

5. **Enhanced Sustainability**: BIM and other design tools help teams optimize building performance, particularly with respect to energy efficiency, sustainability, and environmental impact. Early-stage collaboration allows architects and engineers to design energy-efficient MEPF systems that work harmoniously with the building's architectural features. As a result, the building's overall performance can be optimized, contributing to sustainability goals.

6. **Reduced Project Risk**: Streamlined workflows and real-time coordination reduce the risks associated with building projects, such as schedule delays, cost overruns, and design conflicts. By identifying potential issues early and resolving them collaboratively, integrated workflows help ensure that the project progresses smoothly and successfully.

**Conclusion**

Design workflows and coordination tools are essential for modern building design and construction, enabling greater collaboration, communication, and efficiency. BIM, along with other specialized tools like Navisworks, AutoCAD MEP, and cloud-based platforms, allows for seamless coordination between architects, MEPF engineers, and contractors. These tools help detect clashes early, optimize building systems, and streamline the design process, resulting in cost savings, faster decision-making, and improved project outcomes.

As the complexity of buildings continues to grow and the need for sustainability and efficiency increases, these tools will play a critical role in shaping the future of the AEC industry.

# CHAPTER TEN

# Case Studies of Successful Integration

The concept of integrated building design—where architects, MEPF (Mechanical, Electrical, Plumbing, and fire protection) engineers collaborate from the outset of the project—has proven itself to be a powerful approach in the design and construction of high-performance buildings. This chapter explores **real-world case studies** where integrated design has been successfully implemented, showcasing the tangible benefits of early-stage collaboration between architects and MEPF engineers.

Case studies not only demonstrate the practical application of integrated design principles but also provide insights into the challenges and strategies that were used to overcome them. By examining these examples, we can better understand how integrated design leads to improved energy efficiency, reduced costs, enhanced functionality, and overall better project outcomes.

**1. Introduction to Successful Integrated Design Projects**

The application of integrated design strategies has become a standard practice in the industry, especially in projects where sustainability, efficiency, and performance are top priorities. These projects range from commercial office buildings to residential complexes and even institutional facilities. In every case, the key to success lies in the early and continuous collaboration between architects and MEPF engineers, along with the use of advanced technologies like Building Information Modelling (BIM).

The case studies included in this chapter represent a cross-section of industries and building types. Each case offers valuable lessons and best practices that can be applied to future projects. In analysing these case studies, we will look at the following aspects:

- **Challenges faced** during the project and how they were addressed
- **Integrated strategies** used to optimize systems and ensure collaboration
- **Results achieved** in terms of energy efficiency, cost savings, and overall performance

Let's dive into three different examples of successful integrated design in real-world projects: a **commercial office building**, a **residential complex**, and a **healthcare facility**.

**Case Study 1: The Edge – Amsterdam, Netherlands**

**Project Overview:**

- **Building Type**: Commercial Office Building
- **Location**: Amsterdam, Netherlands
- **Size**: 40,000 square meters (430,556 square feet)
- **Architect**: PLP Architecture
- **MEPF Engineers**: Arup
- **Sustainability Certification**: BREEAM Outstanding

The Edge in Amsterdam is one of the most famous examples of a successful integrated design project. This **smart building** incorporates advanced technology and sustainable features while also utilizing the principles of integrated design to optimize the building's MEPF systems. The building's design focuses on **energy efficiency**, **sustainability**, and creating a comfortable, productive environment for its occupants.

**Challenges:**

- The Edge had to be designed with energy efficiency and sustainability as core priorities.
- The building needed to incorporate advanced **smart building technologies** while maintaining the architectural aesthetics and functionality.
- Coordination between the building's advanced technological systems, its MEPF infrastructure, and the architectural design had to be flawless to ensure seamless integration.

**Integrated Design Strategies:**

- **Early Collaboration**: The project began with early-stage collaboration between architects and MEPF engineers. The design team used BIM to develop a comprehensive model, allowing the integration of systems such as HVAC, lighting, electrical, and fire protection from the start.
- **Energy-Efficient HVAC System**: The HVAC system was optimized for the building's needs using smart technology. The system utilizes **thermal energy storage** and advanced sensors to provide cooling and heating based on real-time occupancy and environmental conditions.
- **Smart Lighting**: The building features **LED lighting** that is connected to an occupancy-based control system. Lights automatically adjust based on daylight levels and occupancy patterns, optimizing energy use.
- **Building Management System (BMS)**: A centralized BMS integrates all building systems, allowing for real-time monitoring and adjustments. This helps optimize energy consumption across the building, reducing waste and improving efficiency.
- **Sustainability Features**: The Edge is designed to be energy-neutral. It uses **solar panels** for renewable energy generation, and the building's insulation, orientation, and windows were optimized for energy conservation.

**Results Achieved:**

- **Energy Efficiency**: The building's smart systems contribute to a 70% reduction in energy consumption compared to a traditional office building.
- **Cost Savings**: The early-stage collaboration between architects and MEPF engineers resulted in a more efficient design that reduced operating costs.
- **Sustainability**: The Edge is one of the world's greenest office buildings, with a **BREEAM Outstanding**certification, the highest rating for sustainable design.
- **User Experience**: The integration of smart technologies improved comfort and productivity for the building's occupants, allowing them to adjust lighting, temperature, and other settings according to their preferences.

**Lessons Learned:**

- The early integration of smart building systems and energy-efficient MEPF designs helped meet the project's sustainability goals.
- BIM and collaborative workflows played a crucial role in ensuring the smooth integration of complex systems.
- Real-time data from smart systems allowed for continuous optimization and monitoring of building performance.

**Case Study 2: Bosco Verticale (Vertical Forest) – Milan, Italy**
**Project Overview:**

- **Building Type:** Residential Complex
- **Location:** Milan, Italy
- **Size:** Two towers, 80 and 112 meters in height
- **Architect:** Stefano Boeri Architetti
- **MEPF Engineers:** Studio Tecnico Ingenieros Associati (STIA)
- **Sustainability Certification:** LEED Gold

The **Bosco Verticale**, or "Vertical Forest," is a unique residential complex in Milan, Italy, known for its **green design** and integration of urban nature. The towers are home to over 9,000 trees and 13,000 plants, making it a pioneering project in sustainable urban development.

**Challenges:**

- Integrating a large number of plants and trees into a residential high-rise required careful coordination between architecture and MEPF systems.
- Ensuring the building's systems supported the health of the plants while maintaining comfort and energy efficiency for residents.
- The vertical nature of the building posed challenges for both **water management** and **HVAC systems**.

**Integrated Design Strategies:**

- **Early Collaboration:** Architects and MEPF engineers collaborated early on to design a building that would incorporate both green elements and sustainable technologies. The use of BIM allowed the teams to integrate the complex systems of the plant irrigation system, HVAC, plumbing, and lighting.

- **Water Management System**: A comprehensive **irrigation system** was designed to support the plants on the building's balconies and facades. The system collects rainwater and recycles water from the building's wastewater to nourish the greenery. MEPF engineers worked closely with the architects to integrate the irrigation system into the building design while maintaining aesthetic integrity.
- **Energy-Efficient HVAC and Heating**: The building utilizes a **geothermal heat pump** system that provides both heating and cooling. The system is designed to optimize energy consumption, using the thermal mass of the building and the surrounding landscape to moderate internal temperatures.
- **Smart Lighting**: The lighting system adjusts based on natural daylight levels and occupancy. LED lights throughout the building are connected to sensors that minimize energy use.

**Results Achieved:**

- **Sustainability**: Bosco Verticale received the **LEED Gold** certification for its sustainable design, which incorporates energy-efficient systems, green roofs, and a strong focus on water conservation.
- **Energy Efficiency**: The building consumes far less energy than traditional high-rise buildings, thanks to its use of geothermal heating and cooling, along with the natural shading provided by the plants.
- **Improved Air Quality**: The trees and plants play a key role in improving air quality by absorbing $CO_2$, producing oxygen, and reducing urban heat island effects.
- **Social Impact**: The Vertical Forest provides residents with an innovative living environment that promotes interaction with nature, improving overall quality of life.

**Lessons Learned:**

- Early-stage collaboration between architects and MEPF engineers was essential in designing the irrigation and energy systems that supported the building's greenery.
- The integration of sustainable systems with the building's unique design allowed for energy savings and reduced environmental impact.

- Green infrastructure, when designed and integrated effectively, can provide numerous benefits beyond aesthetics, including improved air quality and reduced energy consumption.

**Case Study 3: St. Michael's Hospital – Toronto, Canada**
**Project Overview:**

- **Building Type**: Healthcare Facility
- **Location**: Toronto, Canada
- **Size**: 1 million square feet
- **Architect**: Diamond Schmitt Architects
- **MEPF Engineers**: Crossey Engineering Ltd.
- **Sustainability Certification**: LEED Platinum

St. Michael's Hospital in Toronto is a prominent example of successful integrated design in the healthcare sector. The project involved the construction of a large, state-of-the-art healthcare facility with a focus on **sustainability, energy efficiency**, and **operational performance**.

**Challenges:**

- The hospital's systems had to be optimized for **energy efficiency** while maintaining the high-performance requirements needed for medical facilities, such as ventilation, air quality, and medical gas distribution.
- Integrating the needs of healthcare operations with the building's systems required close coordination to ensure that critical systems like HVAC, lighting, and water supply were highly reliable.
- The design had to meet strict **healthcare facility standards** while also integrating sustainable building systems.

**Integrated Design Strategies:**

- **Early Collaboration**: St. Michael's Hospital is a great example of how MEPF engineers worked closely with architects from the beginning of the design process to ensure that healthcare standards were met without compromising on sustainability or energy efficiency.
- **Energy-Efficient HVAC Systems**: The HVAC system was designed to meet the specific needs of a healthcare facility, ensuring that the hospital had the right levels of ventilation and air quality while using **high-**

**efficiency systems.**

- **Integrated Energy Solutions**: The hospital uses **high-efficiency boilers, chillers**, and **heat recovery systems** to reduce energy consumption. The building also incorporates **solar panels** and other renewable energy technologies to reduce its reliance on the grid.
- **Water Conservation**: Water-saving systems, such as low-flow fixtures and an efficient **rainwater harvesting system**, were incorporated into the hospital's plumbing design.

**Results Achieved:**

- **Energy Efficiency**: The hospital has achieved **LEED Platinum** certification for its energy-efficient systems, sustainable materials, and water conservation strategies.
- **Reduced Operating Costs**: The building's operational efficiency is enhanced by the energy-saving systems, including efficient HVAC, lighting, and water systems.
- **Improved Occupant Comfort**: The building provides a comfortable and safe environment for patients, staff, and visitors, thanks to the optimized HVAC and lighting systems.
- **Sustainability**: The hospital's use of renewable energy, efficient systems, and sustainable materials reduces its environmental impact and operational costs.

**Lessons Learned:**

- Close collaboration between architects and MEPF engineers is crucial for integrating healthcare-specific systems while ensuring sustainability and energy efficiency.
- Healthcare facilities require highly reliable systems that can maintain optimal performance at all times, and early-stage collaboration ensures that these requirements are met.
- Energy efficiency and sustainability are achievable in healthcare facilities without compromising on functionality or patient care.

## Conclusion

The case studies explored in this chapter provide real-world examples of how integrated design principles can lead to more sustainable, efficient, and high-performing buildings. Early-stage collaboration between architects, MEPF engineers, and other stakeholders ensures that all systems are designed to work together seamlessly, reducing costs, improving performance, and creating buildings that are more comfortable and energy-efficient.

From office buildings to healthcare facilities to residential complexes, the benefits of integrated design are clear. These projects highlight the importance of collaboration, the use of advanced technologies like BIM, and the integration of sustainability and energy efficiency measures. The lessons learned from these projects can serve as a guide for future integrated design projects, ensuring that the built environment continues to evolve toward greater performance and sustainability.

# CHAPTER ELEVEN

# Sustainability and Green Building Certifications

As global concerns about climate change, energy consumption, and environmental degradation rise, the demand for sustainable buildings has reached new heights. In response to these concerns, building design has evolved to place a significant emphasis on **sustainability** and **green building certifications**. These certifications serve as a standard for measuring a building's environmental performance and the effectiveness of its design in areas like energy efficiency, water conservation, indoor environmental quality, and the use of sustainable materials.

Sustainability in building design is not just about reducing energy use; it is about creating buildings that minimize their environmental footprint while improving the health and comfort of their occupants. Achieving sustainability requires a coordinated approach, where architects, MEPF engineers, contractors, and other stakeholders work together from the beginning to design systems that are energy-efficient, cost-effective, and environmentally friendly.

In this chapter, we will explore the **principles of sustainability**, discuss the **most widely recognized green building certifications** such as **LEED, BREEAM,IGBC** and **GRIHA,** and examine how integrated design plays a critical role in helping buildings achieve sustainability and green certification goals.

### 1. Introduction to Sustainability in Building Design

Sustainable building design focuses on reducing the impact of construction and building operations on the environment. This includes:

- **Energy efficiency**: Using less energy for heating, cooling, lighting, and other building systems.

- **Water conservation**: Reducing water consumption through efficient plumbing fixtures, rainwater harvesting, and wastewater reuse systems.
- **Use of sustainable materials**: Choosing materials that have a low environmental impact, are renewable, and are sourced responsibly.
- **Indoor environmental quality**: Ensuring healthy air quality, natural lighting, and acoustics that promote the well-being of building occupants.

As the environmental impacts of construction and the operation of buildings have become more apparent, there has been an increased push to design and construct buildings that not only minimize their carbon footprint but also contribute positively to the surrounding environment. Sustainable design practices also focus on long-term efficiency, ensuring that buildings continue to function in a way that supports sustainability goals throughout their lifecycle.

The focus on sustainability in building design is critical for reducing the construction industry's overall environmental impact. According to the World Green Building Council, buildings account for approximately **39% of global carbon emissions**, making green building strategies an essential part of global efforts to mitigate climate change.

## 2. The Role of Integrated Design in Sustainability

Integrated design is a crucial component of sustainable building design because it fosters collaboration among all stakeholders from the very beginning of the project. The early involvement of architects, MEPF engineers, structural engineers, and contractors in an integrated design process ensures that sustainability goals are embedded into the project from the outset.

In integrated design, each team member brings their expertise to the table, enabling the development of more efficient, coordinated, and sustainable systems. For example, an architect may design a building that maximizes natural daylight to reduce reliance on artificial lighting. MEPF engineers can then design an energy-efficient lighting system that complements the natural light strategy, while also ensuring that HVAC systems work efficiently with the building's envelope to reduce energy consumption.

Here's how early-stage collaboration leads to sustainability:

- **Optimized energy use**: Collaboration ensures that energy-efficient systems are appropriately sized and implemented in the building's design. Integrated design reduces waste in heating, cooling, and lighting while considering energy-saving technologies such as **solar panels**, **geothermal energy**, and **high-performance insulation**.
- **Water management**: Plumbing engineers can help design water-efficient systems that align with the architectural vision, such as low-flow fixtures, greywater reuse, or rainwater harvesting systems.
- **Materials selection**: Early collaboration helps identify sustainable materials that meet both aesthetic and performance criteria. For example, architects and engineers can jointly evaluate the environmental impacts of construction materials, prioritizing recycled content, locally sourced materials, or those with low environmental footprints.
- **Indoor environmental quality**: Integrated design improves the indoor air quality of the building, ensuring that HVAC, ventilation, and filtration systems are well-designed to enhance the health and comfort of the building's occupants.

Through integrated design, sustainability is not merely an add-on to a project but becomes a central focus throughout the building's lifecycle, from planning and design to construction and operation.

**3. Green Building Certifications**

Green building certifications provide a standardized way to evaluate and recognize buildings that meet high sustainability standards. These certifications are awarded based on a building's performance in several key areas, such as energy and water efficiency, waste reduction, and occupant health and comfort.

Here are the most recognized green building certification systems:

1.  **LEED (Leadership in Energy and Environmental Design):**

**Overview:**

- **Developed by**: U.S. Green Building Council (USGBC)
- **Established**: 1998
- **Primary Focus**: Energy efficiency, sustainability, and environmental responsibility

- **Global Reach**: LEED is the most widely recognized green building certification in the world, with projects in over 160 countries.
- **Categories**: LEED evaluates buildings in several categories, including energy use, water efficiency, air quality, materials, and site impact.

**Rating System**: LEED uses a **point-based rating system**, where projects earn points for meeting specific criteria in each category. The total number of points determines the level of certification:

- **Certified** (40–49 points)
- **Silver** (50–59 points)
- **Gold** (60–79 points)
- **Platinum** (80+ points)

The criteria are divided into various sections that assess a building's performance in different aspects of sustainability:

1. **Sustainable Sites (SS)**: This category assesses the environmental impact of the building site and encourages responsible land use. Projects can earn points for things like reducing impervious surfaces, managing stormwater runoff, and enhancing the building's connectivity to public transportation.
2. **Water Efficiency (WE)**: LEED promotes water-saving measures such as low-flow fixtures, water-efficient landscaping, and greywater recycling.
3. **Energy and Atmosphere (EA)**: This section evaluates energy efficiency and the reduction of greenhouse gas emissions. It includes requirements for high-performance HVAC systems, lighting, and renewable energy sources like solar or wind power.
4. **Materials and Resources (MR)**: The MR category encourages the use of sustainable, recycled, and locally sourced building materials. It also addresses waste management during construction and the life cycle of the materials used in the building.
5. **Indoor Environmental Quality (IEQ)**: This category evaluates how well the building provides a healthy, comfortable, and productive environment for its occupants. It considers air quality, lighting, acoustics, and thermal comfort.
6. **Innovation in Design (ID)**: Points are awarded for innovative design strategies that go beyond the typical requirements and contribute to the

overall sustainability of the building.

7. **Regional Priority (RP)**: This category provides additional points for addressing specific environmental concerns that are relevant to the building's geographical location.

**Benefits of LEED:**

- **Energy and Cost Savings**: LEED buildings consume less energy, resulting in lower utility bills for building owners and tenants.
- **Increased Property Value**: LEED certification can increase the building's market value and attract environmentally conscious tenants.
- **Enhanced Occupant Health**: LEED buildings provide better indoor air quality and lighting, leading to healthier and more productive occupants.
- **Environmental Impact**: LEED-certified buildings significantly reduce energy consumption and carbon emissions, contributing to global sustainability goals.

  - **Categories**: LEED evaluates buildings based on several key performance areas:

    - **Sustainable Sites**: Impact on the environment, land use, and ecology.
    - **Water Efficiency**: Reduction of water use and impact on water resources.
    - **Energy and Atmosphere**: Efficient use of energy and use of renewable energy sources.
    - **Materials and Resources**: Use of sustainable, recycled, and responsibly sourced materials.
    - **Indoor Environmental Quality**: Improved air quality, natural lighting, and thermal comfort.
    - **Innovation**: Innovative strategies and solutions.
    - **Regional Priority**: Credits specific to the regional area's environmental issues.

  - **LEED Certification Levels**: There are four levels of certification: **Certified, Silver, Gold, and Platinum**. Platinum is the highest level and is reserved for projects that achieve exemplary performance across all categories.

**Case Example**: Many commercial office buildings and institutional projects across the world have achieved **LEED Gold** or **Platinum** certification by integrating sustainable design features such as high-performance glazing, energy-efficient HVAC systems, and renewable energy sources like solar panels.

1. **BREEAM (Building Research Establishment Environmental Assessment Method):**

**Overview:** Building Research Establishment (BRE) Developed in the UK, **BREEAM** is one of the world's oldest and most widely used green building certification systems.

- **Established**: 1990
- **Primary Focus**: Environmental sustainability, focusing on energy use, waste reduction, and environmental impact
- **Global Reach**: BREEAM is a leading certification in the UK and is also widely used in Europe and around the world.

**Rating System:** BREEAM uses a points-based system to evaluate buildings across multiple categories. The final score determines the certification level:

- **Pass** (30–44 points)
- **Good** (45–59 points)
- **Very Good** (60–74 points)
- **Excellent** (75–89 points)
- **Outstanding** (90+ points)

Key categories in the BREEAM rating system include:

1. **Energy**: BREEAM promotes energy efficiency by requiring buildings to meet certain energy-saving standards. This includes reducing the building's carbon footprint, improving insulation, and optimizing heating, cooling, and lighting systems.
2. **Water**: Water conservation is a key focus, with requirements for low-water-use fixtures, rainwater harvesting, and efficient irrigation systems.

3. **Materials**: BREEAM encourages the use of sustainable materials that have a low environmental impact and are sourced responsibly.
4. **Waste**: The waste category assesses how well the building minimizes waste during construction and operation, including recycling and waste management systems.
5. **Pollution**: BREEAM evaluates the building's impact on the surrounding environment, including air and water pollution, as well as noise reduction.
6. **Health and Wellbeing**: This category considers the comfort and health of building occupants, including indoor air quality, access to natural light, and thermal comfort.
7. **Innovation**: Innovative strategies that contribute to sustainability are awarded additional points.

**Benefits of BREEAM:**

- **Sustainability**: BREEAM-certified buildings have lower environmental impact, contributing to energy conservation, waste reduction, and healthier indoor environments.
- **Global Recognition**: BREEAM is widely recognized in Europe and is gaining traction in other parts of the world, making it a valuable certification for international projects.
- **Market Advantage**: BREEAM certification can enhance a building's reputation, attracting tenants, investors, and buyers interested in sustainable properties.

  - **Categories**: BREEAM evaluates buildings across several categories, including:

    - **Energy**: Energy consumption and management.
    - **Water**: Water efficiency and use.
    - **Health and Wellbeing**: Impact on occupant health and comfort.
    - **Materials**: Sustainable material sourcing and impact.
    - **Waste**: Waste reduction and management.
    - **Pollution**: Reducing environmental pollution.
    - **Innovation**: Innovative approaches to sustainability.

○ **BREEAM Rating Levels**: BREEAM uses a points-based system, with ratings ranging from **Pass** to **Outstanding**. Buildings achieve higher ratings by implementing more sustainable measures and meeting higher environmental standards.

**Case Example**: The **The Crystal** in London is an example of a BREEAM Outstanding certified building. It features a combination of **green roofs**, **solar power**, and **rainwater harvesting**, and is designed to be energy-efficient, reducing both operational costs and environmental impact.

3. **IGBC (Indian Green Building Council):**

**Overview:** Indian Green Building Council (IGBC) **IGBC** is the Indian counterpart to LEED and provides green building ratings for buildings in India. It is recognized as a key certification system in the region and focuses on energy efficiency, water conservation, and the use of sustainable materials.

- **Established**: 2001
- **Primary Focus**: Sustainable building design in India, addressing the unique environmental and regional challenges of the country
- **Regional Focus**: IGBC is the leading green building certification system in India, with a growing presence in the South Asian region.

**Rating System:** IGBC provides several certification levels based on the building's performance:

- **Certified**
- **Silver**
- **Gold**
- **Platinum**

Key categories in IGBC certification include:

1. **Sustainable Sites**: This category promotes responsible site selection, minimizing environmental impact, and promoting access to public transportation.

2. **Water Conservation**: Efficient water management systems, including rainwater harvesting, water-efficient fixtures, and wastewater treatment, are encouraged.
3. **Energy Efficiency**: IGBC promotes energy-efficient building systems, including HVAC optimization, renewable energy integration, and building envelope enhancements.
4. **Material Usage**: IGBC encourages the use of sustainable, low-impact materials that are locally sourced, recyclable, and environmentally friendly.
5. **Indoor Environmental Quality**: Good indoor air quality, natural lighting, and comfortable thermal conditions are prioritized for occupant health and well-being.
6. **Innovation**: Points are awarded for innovative strategies that enhance sustainability and provide solutions tailored to the local environment.
7. **Health and Wellbeing**: This category ensures that the design improves the quality of life for occupants, with considerations for air quality, lighting, acoustics, and access to nature.

**Benefits of IGBC:**

- **Energy and Water Savings**: IGBC-certified buildings use energy more efficiently, resulting in reduced operational costs.
- **Environmental Stewardship**: By addressing local environmental issues, IGBC contributes to sustainability in the Indian context.
- **Economic Advantages**: Green buildings typically experience higher demand and can command higher rental values, making them financially attractive for developers.

**Categories**: IGBC evaluates buildings in the following categories:

- **Energy Efficiency**: Reduction in energy use and integration of renewable energy sources.
- **Water Efficiency**: Water-saving measures and efficient plumbing systems.
- **Materials and Resources**: Use of sustainable, recyclable, and eco-friendly materials.
- **Indoor Environmental Quality**: Impact on indoor air quality, lighting, and acoustics.

- **Innovation**: Creative sustainability solutions tailored to the local context.

- **IGBC Rating Levels**: IGBC offers ratings such as **Certified, Silver, Gold**, and **Platinum** for buildings that achieve various levels of sustainable performance.

**Case Example**: The **Bangalore International Airport** achieved **IGBC Gold** certification by integrating energy-efficient systems, water conservation practices, and sustainable construction materials.

## 4. GRIHA (Green Rating for Integrated Habitat Assessment)

**Overview:** The Energy and Resources Institute (TERI) in collaboration with the Ministry of New and Renewable Energy (MNRE), Government of India

- **Established:** 2007
- **Primary Focus:** Sustainability with a focus on reducing resource consumption and promoting energy-efficient design in Indian buildings

**Rating System:** GRIHA provides a five-star rating system based on the building's performance across several categories:

- **Site Planning and Selection:** Reduces the impact on the natural environment and promotes sustainable urban development.
- **Energy Efficiency:** Encourages the use of energy-efficient technologies and renewable energy sources.
- **Water Conservation:** Includes strategies for efficient water use and waste reduction.
- **Indoor Environmental Quality:** Focuses on the health and comfort of occupants by providing proper lighting, ventilation, and air quality.
- **Materials and Resources:** Promotes sustainable material selection, waste management, and resource conservation.
- **Innovation:** Rewards innovative sustainable solutions that go beyond the basic requirements

## 4. The Benefits of Green Building Certifications

The adoption of green building certifications provides a variety of benefits to building owners, occupants, and the environment. These benefits include:

1. **Energy and Operational Cost Savings**: Green buildings are designed to be energy-efficient, resulting in lower utility costs for building owners and occupants. The incorporation of energy-efficient HVAC systems, LED lighting, and renewable energy technologies like solar panels can lead to significant long-term savings. For example, the **Edge** in Amsterdam reduces its energy consumption by 70% compared to conventional office buildings.

2. **Improved Occupant Health and Productivity**: Green buildings focus not only on environmental impact but also on the health and comfort of their occupants. Higher indoor air quality, better lighting conditions, access to natural elements, and reduced exposure to harmful materials contribute to better occupant health, satisfaction, and productivity. Studies have shown that employees in green buildings report higher levels of satisfaction and productivity.

3. **Environmental Impact Reduction**: Sustainable buildings help mitigate the effects of climate change by reducing energy consumption, lowering carbon emissions, and conserving water. By minimizing the impact of construction and building operations, green buildings contribute to global sustainability efforts. For example, LEED-certified buildings are designed to reduce their **carbon footprint** and waste production.

4. **Increased Property Value**: Sustainable, energy-efficient buildings are increasingly sought after in the real estate market. Buildings with green certifications often command higher rents, attract premium tenants, and have higher resale values. For example, buildings with **LEED Platinum** certification are recognized for their sustainable features, attracting high-quality tenants willing to pay for the benefits of a green building.

5. **Market Differentiation**: Achieving green building certifications allows developers and building owners to differentiate their properties in the marketplace. Certification provides a competitive edge and enhances the reputation of the building, attracting environmentally conscious tenants and investors.

**Conclusion**

Sustainability and green building certifications have become essential in the modern construction industry. As the demand for more environmentally responsible and energy-efficient buildings grows, integrated design strategies and green building certifications like LEED, BREEAM, IGBC and GRIHA will continue to play a key role in shaping the future of the built environment.

By incorporating sustainable design principles from the outset and working collaboratively across disciplines, architects and MEPF engineers can create buildings that are not only efficient and cost-effective but also contribute to the health and well-being of occupants and the planet. The case studies and benefits discussed in this chapter highlight the importance of sustainability in building design and demonstrate the significant advantages of pursuing green building certifications.

# CHAPTER TWELVE

# Smart Buildings and Emerging Technologies

The concept of smart buildings has evolved significantly in recent years, transforming the way we think about building design, construction, and operation. A **smart building** is one that uses **advanced technologies** to enhance the comfort, efficiency, safety, and sustainability of the environment. These technologies are deeply integrated with the **Mechanical, Electrical, Plumbing (MEPF), and Fire Protection (F)** systems, creating a cohesive environment where data-driven decisions can optimize building performance. This chapter will explore the integration of **smart technologies** in modern building design, focusing on **emerging technologies**, the **Internet of Things (IoT), Artificial Intelligence (AI)**, and their role in transforming buildings into high-performing, efficient, and sustainable spaces.

We will look into the **core components** of smart buildings, the **benefits** they offer, how **MEPF systems** are integrated with these technologies, and the **future of smart buildings** in the context of **emerging technologies**.

**1. Introduction to Smart Buildings**

A smart building is a structure that uses **sensors, automation systems,** and **advanced software** to collect data, control various systems, and improve the building's operational performance. These buildings are equipped with technologies that enable real-time monitoring and management of various systems such as **HVAC, lighting, security, energy consumption,** and more. The main goal of a smart building is to provide a more **efficient, sustainable,** and **comfortable environment** for its occupants, while also lowering operational costs and energy consumption.

**Smart Building Features Include:**

- **Automation**: The ability to automatically adjust systems like lighting, heating, cooling, and ventilation based on real-time data from sensors.
- **Energy Management**: The integration of **smart meters** and **energy-efficient systems** to monitor and control energy consumption.
- **Lighting Control**: **LED lights** connected to sensors that adjust based on occupancy or daylight levels.
- **Occupant Comfort**: Automated systems that monitor and adjust temperature, humidity, and air quality to create an optimal environment.
- **Security**: Advanced security systems using **biometrics**, **smart locks**, **facial recognition**, and **surveillance** integrated with the building management system (BMS).

By integrating these technologies, smart buildings can automatically respond to environmental changes, provide real-time data to building managers, and even adapt to occupants' behaviours and preferences.

### 2. Core Technologies of Smart Buildings

At the heart of every smart building lies a set of advanced technologies that enable seamless coordination and intelligent automation. These technologies work together to optimize building performance, reduce operational costs, and enhance occupant satisfaction. Key technologies include:

### A. Internet of Things (IoT)

The **Internet of Things (IoT)** refers to the network of physical devices—such as sensors, actuators, smart meters, and appliances—that communicate with each other and the cloud over the internet. In smart buildings, IoT devices are embedded into various building systems to monitor and control activities, such as lighting, heating, cooling, security, and energy usage.

- **Smart Sensors**: Devices that collect data on occupancy, temperature, humidity, light levels, $CO_2$ concentration, and more. This data is used to optimize system operations.
- **Smart Meters**: Devices that track energy usage in real-time and can communicate with building management systems (BMS) to optimize energy consumption.
- **Building Management System (BMS)**: The central control platform that integrates all IoT-enabled devices, collects data, and makes real-time decisions to optimize building performance.

By connecting various building systems to the internet and allowing them to communicate, IoT technologies make it possible to monitor and control a building's performance remotely.

**B. Artificial Intelligence (AI) and Machine Learning (ML)**

**AI** and **Machine Learning (ML)** have become integral to the optimization of smart building systems. These technologies use **data analytics** to predict patterns and automate responses. They enable buildings to become **self-learning**, improving their performance based on historical data and real-time inputs.

- **Predictive Analytics**: AI algorithms can predict the energy consumption patterns of a building and adjust the HVAC and lighting systems accordingly, improving energy efficiency.
- **Fault Detection and Diagnosis**: AI can detect system faults early by analysing trends and anomalies in building data. This helps reduce downtime and maintenance costs.
- **Occupant Behaviour Modelling**: AI can learn occupants' preferences for temperature, lighting, and other conditions, enabling buildings to automatically adjust these parameters for optimal comfort.

AI and ML not only improve operational efficiency but also contribute to sustainability by enabling **demand-response systems**, which automatically adjust energy use in response to grid conditions or peak load times.

**C. Automation and Control Systems**

Automation plays a central role in smart buildings. It involves using **programmable systems, sensors,** and **actuators** to control the operation of various systems within a building.

- **Lighting Control: Dimmable lighting** systems and **motion sensors** automatically adjust the lighting levels based on occupancy and daylight availability.
- **HVAC Automation**: Temperature, humidity, and air quality are controlled automatically by HVAC systems, which are programmed to maintain optimal conditions based on real-time data.
- **Smart Ventilation**: Using $CO_2$ sensors to monitor air quality and adjust ventilation rates, ensuring that the building is both energy-efficient and comfortable for occupants.

Automation systems not only improve building efficiency but also enhance comfort by continuously adapting to environmental changes.

**D. Energy Management Systems (EMS)**

Energy management is a critical function of smart buildings. **Energy Management Systems (EMS)** help optimize the building's energy use by collecting data on energy consumption, identifying inefficiencies, and making adjustments to reduce energy waste.

- **Real-Time Monitoring**: EMS allows building managers to monitor energy consumption in real time, identifying areas where energy is being wasted.
- **Demand Response**: EMS can automatically adjust the building's energy usage in response to changes in energy supply or grid demand. For example, during peak hours, EMS can lower the energy load by adjusting HVAC settings, lighting, and other non-essential systems.
- **Energy Storage**: Some smart buildings incorporate **energy storage systems** (like **batteries** or **thermal storage**) that store excess energy during low-demand periods and use it during peak demand, reducing reliance on the grid.

EMS can significantly reduce operational costs while making buildings more sustainable by minimizing their carbon footprint.

**3. Integration of MEPF Systems with Smart Technologies**

A building's **Mechanical, Electrical, Plumbing (MEPF)** systems are crucial to its overall performance, and integrating these systems with smart technologies is key to creating a truly smart building. The integration of IoT, AI, and automation into MEPF systems improves **efficiency**, **comfort**, **safety**, and **sustainability**.

**A. HVAC Integration**

- **Smart Thermostats**: Smart thermostats, such as **Nest** or **Ecobee**, learn occupant behaviour and adjust the heating and cooling systems to maintain comfort while optimizing energy use.
- **Variable Air Volume (VAV)** Systems: VAV systems adjust airflow based on occupancy or environmental conditions. When integrated with IoT devices, these systems can optimize temperature and air quality in real time, providing better control over energy usage.

- **Geothermal and Heat Pumps**: Smart buildings can integrate renewable energy sources like **geothermal heat pumps** and **solar panels**, which are controlled by an AI-driven system to ensure optimal energy use and minimal waste.

### B. Lighting Integration

- **Smart Lighting Systems**: Integration with IoT sensors enables lighting systems to adjust automatically based on occupancy, time of day, and ambient light levels. These systems can be controlled remotely, and AI can predict lighting needs based on past behaviour, minimizing energy use while providing optimal lighting conditions.
- **Daylight Harvesting**: Using **sensors** to measure the amount of natural light entering the building, systems can adjust artificial lighting to maintain consistent lighting levels. This reduces reliance on artificial lighting and contributes to energy savings.

### C. Plumbing Integration

- **Water Efficiency**: Smart plumbing systems integrate **water-saving fixtures** (such as **low-flow faucets** and **toilets**) with sensors to monitor water use and detect leaks. **Water meters** can provide real-time data on water consumption, allowing for adjustments to minimize waste.
- **Greywater Recycling**: Smart buildings can integrate **greywater recycling systems**, which treat and reuse water from sinks, showers, and washing machines for non-potable applications, such as irrigation or toilet flushing.
- **Leak Detection**: IoT sensors can detect leaks in plumbing systems and send alerts to building managers, reducing water waste and preventing potential damage.

### D. Fire Protection and Security Integration

- **Smart Fire Detection**: Fire protection systems in smart buildings integrate advanced sensors, such as smoke, heat, and CO detectors, that are connected to a central monitoring system. These systems can send real-time alerts to building management and emergency responders, improving response time.

- **Automated Fire Suppression Systems**: In addition to traditional sprinklers, smart buildings may include **dry chemical fire suppression systems** that are triggered based on real-time data. AI can also predict fire risks based on environmental data, providing early warnings.
- **Smart Security Systems**: Integration with IoT-based **access control systems, smart locks,** and **facial recognition** ensures higher security levels. Smart surveillance systems with real-time data analysis improve security monitoring and incident detection.

### 4. Benefits of Smart Buildings and Emerging Technologies

Smart buildings equipped with emerging technologies offer a variety of benefits that improve building performance, occupant comfort, and operational efficiency.

### A. Increased Energy Efficiency

- Smart buildings are designed to minimize energy consumption through real-time monitoring and adaptive systems. Automated lighting, HVAC systems, and energy-efficient appliances work together to reduce the building's overall energy demand.
- By using **renewable energy sources** like **solar power** or **wind energy**, smart buildings can generate their own energy, further reducing reliance on the grid.

### B. Improved Comfort and Productivity

- Occupant comfort is enhanced by maintaining optimal temperature, lighting, and air quality levels. **AI-driven systems** adjust settings based on user preferences, while **smart sensors** ensure that spaces are neither too hot nor too cold.
- Studies have shown that smart buildings contribute to **higher productivity** and **well-being** among occupants. By optimizing environmental conditions, smart buildings foster a healthier and more comfortable work or living environment.

### C. Reduced Operational Costs

- **Energy management systems** (EMS) and **demand-response technologies** allow building owners to control energy usage efficiently, resulting in significant savings over time.

- **Automated maintenance** and **predictive analytics** reduce the need for costly repairs and unplanned downtime by identifying issues before they escalate.

### D. Sustainability

- Smart buildings contribute to environmental sustainability by reducing **carbon emissions, energy consumption**, and **water usage**. They also encourage the use of **sustainable materials** and **green energy sources**.
- These buildings help achieve **green building certifications** such as **LEED, BREEAM, IGBC** and**GRIHA**, which recognize and reward efforts in environmental performance.

### Conclusion

The future of smart buildings lies in **increased automation, advanced AI, data analytics**, and further integration with the **Internet of Things (IoT)**. As technology evolves, smart buildings will become more intelligent, adaptive, and sustainable.

- **5G Connectivity**: The advent of **5G networks** will provide faster data transmission, enabling real-time communication between smart building systems, improving responsiveness, and enhancing overall system efficiency.
- **Blockchain for Security**: Blockchain could be used for secure and transparent data management in smart buildings, especially in areas like building access control and energy transactions.
- **Autonomous Systems**: Future smart buildings may incorporate **autonomous systems** for building management, including self-optimizing HVAC, lighting, and security systems that learn and adapt without human intervention.

As emerging technologies continue to advance, the potential for creating even more efficient, sustainable, and responsive buildings will expand, contributing to a more connected and environmentally responsible future.

# CHAPTER THIRTEEN

# Project Management and Coordination Techniques

**Project management** is one of the most critical aspects of any building project. A successful project requires the effective coordination of various disciplines, including architecture, MEPF engineering, structural engineering, and contractors. Managing complex workflows, ensuring the timely completion of tasks, and maintaining the project's budget are vital components of successful project execution. The integration of **MEPF systems**, sustainability goals, and evolving technological requirements makes modern building projects more challenging and complex, requiring advanced project management techniques.

In this chapter, we will explore the key **project management** and **coordination** techniques that lead to successful building projects. We will focus on the importance of **early-stage collaboration**, the use of **BIM (Building Information Modelling)**, the role of **technology** in streamlining processes, and the significance of **communication strategies** in ensuring that all project stakeholders are aligned throughout the construction process.

**1. The Importance of Coordination in Project Management**

In any building project, **coordination** among various stakeholders is paramount. The project team typically consists of architects, structural engineers, MEPF engineers, contractors, subcontractors, and owners. These diverse stakeholders must collaborate throughout the design and construction phases to ensure that the project stays on track, on budget, and meets the desired outcomes. Coordination in construction projects goes beyond simple communication; it involves the alignment of each team's goals and responsibilities, ensuring that the various aspects of the project do not conflict or overlap.

The **coordination process** typically includes:

- **Aligning project goals**: All stakeholders must understand and work toward a common vision, ensuring that each discipline's objectives are aligned with the project's overall goals.
- **Defining roles and responsibilities**: Clear roles and responsibilities should be assigned to each team member, minimizing confusion and ensuring accountability.
- **Effective communication**: Continuous, transparent communication is crucial for project success, as it allows teams to share updates, resolve conflicts, and address any potential issues early in the process.
- **Managing project timelines**: Proper coordination helps in managing project milestones, ensuring that tasks are completed on schedule and resources are allocated effectively.

Proper coordination not only leads to smoother project execution but also reduces the risks associated with delays, cost overruns, and scope creep.

**2. Early-Stage Collaboration for Successful Project Execution**

One of the most effective ways to ensure the success of a building project is to engage in **early-stage collaboration** between all stakeholders. In traditional construction projects, various disciplines often work in isolation, which can lead to misaligned designs and increased risk of conflicts during construction. In contrast, **integrated project delivery (IPD)** and **collaborative design processes** allow teams to work together from the beginning, identifying and solving potential issues early in the design process.

**Key Benefits of Early-Stage Collaboration:**

1. **Improved Communication**: Engaging all key stakeholders early in the process ensures that there is no miscommunication about the project goals, objectives, and challenges. Everyone involved is aligned from day one.
2. **Proactive Problem Solving**: With all teams working together, potential conflicts or clashes—such as issues with MEPF system integration or building code compliance—can be identified early, reducing the need for costly revisions later.

3. **Design Efficiency**: Collaboration between architects, MEPF engineers, and contractors allows the design to be optimized for performance, cost, and sustainability from the outset. Systems such as HVAC, plumbing, electrical, and fire protection are considered early in the design, avoiding last-minute changes that can disrupt the project timeline.

4. **Cost Control**: By involving key stakeholders in the early stages of design, the project team can identify cost-effective solutions, reduce waste, and avoid costly revisions, leading to greater control over the budget.

**Best Practices for Early-Stage Collaboration:**

- **Workshops and Charrettes**: Holding early **design charrettes** or workshops that involve key team members encourages brainstorming and collective problem-solving. These sessions help ensure that the design goals are agreed upon by all parties.

- **BIM Integration**: Using **Building Information Modelling (BIM)** to develop the initial design allows all stakeholders to visualize the building in 3D and interact with the model. This enables them to make more informed decisions, detect potential issues, and refine the design collaboratively.

- **Establishing Communication Channels**: Early collaboration also requires setting up efficient communication channels, such as project management platforms or collaborative software tools, to ensure that all stakeholders are up-to-date on the project's status and can easily share feedback and ideas.

**3. The Role of Building Information Modelling (BIM) in Project Management**

**BIM (Building Information Modelling)** has become an indispensable tool in modern building projects. It is a process of creating and managing digital representations of a building's physical and functional characteristics. BIM allows architects, MEPF engineers, and contractors to work on the same 3D model in real-time, providing an integrated approach to building design, construction, and operation.

BIM's role in **project management** and **coordination** can be broken down as follows:

**A. Clash Detection and Conflict Resolution**

One of the most significant benefits of BIM is its ability to detect **clashes** between various building systems—such as MEPF systems, structural elements, and architectural components—before construction begins. In traditional design processes, such clashes are often discovered during the construction phase, leading to delays, rework, and additional costs. With BIM, conflicts are identified early, and the design can be adjusted in real-time to ensure that systems fit together seamlessly.

### B. Real-Time Collaboration

BIM enables **real-time collaboration** between all stakeholders. Architects, engineers, and contractors can simultaneously work on the model, making changes that are immediately visible to all team members. This collaborative environment reduces the risk of miscommunication and helps ensure that all parties are working with the most up-to-date information.

### C. Project Visualization

BIM helps project managers visualize the entire construction process, allowing them to foresee potential challenges and inefficiencies before they occur. The 3D model serves as a comprehensive reference that project managers can use to ensure that the design and construction follow the specified requirements and timelines.

### D. Resource and Scheduling Management

BIM tools can be integrated with **4D** (time) and **5D** (cost) planning systems to enhance scheduling and budget management. By linking the building model with project timelines and budgets, project managers can track progress, anticipate delays, and make adjustments to stay on schedule. This approach also helps in optimizing the use of materials and labour, ensuring that resources are allocated efficiently.

### 4. Technology in Project Management: Tools for Effective Coordination

In addition to BIM, several other technologies are helping streamline project management and coordination in the construction industry. These tools assist in managing tasks, tracking progress, and maintaining real-time communication across teams.

### A. Project Management Software

- **Procore:** Procore is a popular construction management platform that provides tools for managing projects, documents, schedules, budgets, and communication across teams. It helps project managers keep everything organized in one place and ensures that all stakeholders are aligned.

- **Builder trend**: Builder trend is another project management tool that focuses on construction scheduling, budgeting, and communication. It also offers integration with other software tools like BIM, allowing for seamless collaboration.
- **Aconex**: Aconex is a cloud-based construction management platform used for managing documents and workflows, enabling teams to collaborate efficiently. It is particularly beneficial for large-scale projects involving multiple teams.

## B. Mobile Technology

- The use of mobile devices in construction projects has grown significantly, allowing on-site workers to stay connected with project management teams. Project managers can use mobile apps to track construction progress, communicate with contractors, and upload real-time photos and data to ensure that the work is proceeding as planned.

## C. Drones and Drones Data Analytics

- Drones are becoming an increasingly important tool in construction project management. Drones equipped with cameras and sensors can capture real-time images and data from the construction site, providing project managers with accurate, up-to-date information. Drone technology helps monitor progress, perform surveys, and check for any discrepancies from the original plan.

## D. Cloud-Based Platforms for Collaboration

- Cloud-based platforms like **Google Drive**, **Microsoft OneDrive**, and **Dropbox** enable project teams to store and share documents, drawings, and specifications in real-time. These platforms ensure that all stakeholders have access to the most current information, promoting better collaboration.

## 5. Effective Communication Techniques for Coordination

Clear and effective communication is one of the cornerstones of successful project management. In construction projects, communication involves a range of stakeholders, including architects, engineers, contractors, and clients. Coordinating these parties effectively requires a set of structured communication strategies.

## A. Regular Coordination Meetings

- **Kick-off Meetings**: At the beginning of the project, a comprehensive **kick-off meeting** should be held with all stakeholders to establish project goals, timelines, budgets, and communication protocols.
- **Weekly or Bi-weekly Meetings**: Regular meetings help ensure that all stakeholders are aligned with the project's progress and that any issues or concerns are addressed promptly. These meetings should include all team members and allow for open discussion of any challenges.
- **Daily Stand-ups**: For larger projects, daily or frequent "stand-up" meetings can be helpful for discussing the day's tasks, challenges, and any changes to the schedule or scope of work.

## B. Collaborative Tools and Platforms

- **Slack, Microsoft Teams**, and other collaborative tools enable instant communication among project teams. These tools provide chat functions, video conferencing, and file-sharing capabilities, allowing quick resolution of questions or concerns.
- **Shared Document Repositories**: Using platforms like **Procore**, **BIM 360**, or **Google Docs**, all project documents, drawings, and schedules can be accessed by the team in real-time, ensuring everyone has the latest version and updates.

## C. Conflict Resolution Strategies

- In any complex project, conflicts are bound to arise. Project managers should have a clear conflict resolution strategy in place, such as **mediation, compromise,** and **collaborative problem-solving.** Resolving conflicts early prevents them from escalating and affecting the project timeline.

## Conclusion

Successful project management requires a combination of early collaboration, effective coordination, and the right tools. Key techniques for ensuring success in modern construction projects include:

- Early-stage collaboration among all stakeholders, including architects, MEPF engineers, contractors, and clients.
- The use of advanced technologies like BIM, project management software, and IoT to improve communication, streamline workflows, and optimize building systems.
- The application of clear communication strategies, such as regular meetings, collaborative platforms, and conflict resolution techniques.
- Leveraging the power of mobile devices, drones, and real-time data analytics to enhance site management and decision-making.

By adhering to these project management and coordination techniques, building projects can be completed on time, within budget, and with a high level of quality. Integrated project delivery and collaboration between all stakeholders ensure that the building's design, systems, and performance are optimized, delivering the best possible outcomes for both developers and occupants.

# CHAPTER FOURTEEN

# Quality Control and Commissioning

**Quality Control (QC)** and **Commissioning (Cx)** are crucial steps in ensuring the functionality, efficiency, and sustainability of building systems once construction is completed. These processes involve verifying that all systems meet the specified requirements, perform as expected, and are ready for occupancy and operation. For **MEPF systems**(Mechanical, Electrical, Plumbing, and Fire Protection), quality control and commissioning play an essential role in ensuring that each system operates efficiently, reliably, and safely.

In this chapter, we will explore the processes of quality control and commissioning in the context of modern building projects, with a particular focus on the integration of **MEPF systems**. We will also discuss how advanced tools like **BIM (Building Information Modelling)** and **project management software** can enhance these processes. Furthermore, we will examine the importance of thorough testing, system integration, and final walkthroughs to ensure that buildings meet performance standards and regulatory compliance.

### 1. Introduction to Quality Control and Commissioning

**Quality Control** and **Commissioning** are distinct but closely related processes in the construction industry. Both aim to ensure that the building and its systems are constructed and perform according to the original design intent, specifications, and regulatory requirements.

- **Quality Control (QC):** This refers to the systematic processes used to monitor and verify that construction activities, materials, and systems meet the required standards and specifications. QC involves inspections, testing, and documentation throughout the construction phase to ensure that the work complies with all regulations and quality benchmarks.

- **Commissioning (Cx)**: Commissioning is the process of testing, adjusting, and ensuring that all building systems operate as intended. This includes verifying the proper operation of mechanical, electrical, plumbing, and fire protection systems, as well as ensuring that they are integrated correctly and work together as a cohesive whole. The commissioning process typically occurs after the construction phase but before the building is turned over to the client or occupants.

Both QC and commissioning are essential for ensuring that a building performs as expected, is energy-efficient, and provides a comfortable, safe environment for its occupants.

**2. The Quality Control Process in Construction**

Quality Control in construction is an ongoing process that spans the entire duration of a building project, from the initial design through to completion. It includes the following key stages:

**A. Pre-Construction Quality Control**

- **Design Reviews**: QC begins during the design phase with a review of the architectural, structural, and MEPF plans to ensure that they meet both functional requirements and quality standards. This includes reviewing the specifications for building systems, materials, and finishes, ensuring compliance with building codes and regulations, and ensuring that the design is constructible and cost-effective.
- **Material Selection**: Choosing high-quality, durable materials is critical to the success of any construction project. During the pre-construction phase, the QC team ensures that the materials specified for the building are of the required quality and performance standards. This includes verifying the performance characteristics of HVAC equipment, electrical systems, and plumbing materials.
- **Subcontractor Qualification**: Ensuring that subcontractors and suppliers meet the quality standards established for the project is a key part of pre-construction quality control. This includes evaluating their qualifications, experience, and past performance on similar projects.

**B. During Construction Quality Control**

- **On-Site Inspections**: QC personnel perform regular inspections throughout the construction process to verify that the work is being carried out according to the approved plans and specifications. These inspections are done on-site and cover everything from **structural elements** to the **installation of MEPF systems.**
- **Testing and Verifications**: In many cases, specific tests need to be performed to ensure that construction systems are being installed properly. This could include testing electrical circuits, HVAC systems, plumbing fixtures, or fire protection systems for functionality and compliance with safety standards.
- **Documenting Deviations**: If deviations from the original design or quality standards are found, they are documented, and corrective actions are taken. This documentation ensures that all parties are aware of any issues and that they are rectified before proceeding with subsequent work.

**C. Final Quality Control Checks**

- **System Integration and Testing**: The final quality control checks ensure that the building systems are fully integrated. This includes testing and verifying that all MEPF systems—such as the HVAC, plumbing, and electrical systems—are correctly installed, connected, and functioning properly.
- **Punch Lists**: A **punch list** is created at the end of the construction phase, listing all the outstanding issues that need to be addressed before the project is complete. The punch list is typically reviewed by both the construction team and the client to ensure that all required fixes are made.

**3. Commissioning: Ensuring Systems Performance**

While **quality control** focuses on verifying compliance with design specifications and regulations, **commissioning** focuses on verifying that all building systems are functioning as intended. Commissioning is typically performed toward the end of the construction process, just before the building is turned over to the client or occupants.

**A. Commissioning of MEPF Systems**

- **HVAC Commissioning**: The commissioning of HVAC systems ensures that they are installed according to design specifications and operate efficiently. This includes testing air distribution systems, verifying that heating and cooling capacities are met, and ensuring that the systems are integrated with other building systems for optimal performance.
- **Electrical Commissioning**: Electrical systems are tested to ensure that they are properly wired and provide the required levels of voltage, amperage, and safety. This also involves testing electrical panels, emergency backup systems, and lighting systems for proper operation.
- **Plumbing Commissioning**: The plumbing systems are tested for water pressure, drainage performance, and leak prevention. This also includes verifying that water-saving fixtures, such as low-flow toilets and faucets, are installed correctly and perform as expected.
- **Fire Protection Systems Commissioning**: Fire alarm, sprinkler, and emergency lighting systems are thoroughly tested to ensure that they function properly in the event of an emergency. Commissioning of these systems is critical to ensuring the safety of the building's occupants.

## B. The Commissioning Process

The commissioning process is a series of steps that ensure the proper functioning of all building systems. These steps include:

1. **Pre-Commissioning Planning**: This phase involves reviewing design documents, developing commissioning procedures, and ensuring that all necessary equipment and materials are available for testing.
2. **System Functional Testing**: Each system is tested under normal operating conditions to verify its functionality. This includes testing equipment and sensors, checking energy performance, and ensuring that all systems are integrated and responsive to control systems.
3. **System Optimization**: After testing, systems are optimized for energy efficiency and performance. This may involve adjusting set points, fine-tuning system operations, and programming smart technologies like occupancy sensors or automated control systems to maximize efficiency.
4. **Documentation and Handover**: Commissioning culminates in the creation of a comprehensive **commissioning report**, which documents all the tests performed, any issues that were identified, and the corrective actions taken. This documentation is handed over to the building owner to ensure proper operation and ongoing maintenance of

the systems.

### C. Ongoing Commissioning and Re-Commissioning

Commissioning is not a one-time event. Over the life of a building, ongoing monitoring and periodic re-commissioning ensure that systems continue to perform at optimal levels. This is especially important for **HVAC** and **energy management systems**, which can benefit from regular performance reviews to maintain energy efficiency and reduce operational costs.

### 4. The Role of Technology in Quality Control and Commissioning

Advances in **technology** have greatly enhanced the processes of quality control and commissioning in modern building projects. Key technologies that streamline these processes include:

### A. Building Information Modelling (BIM)

- **BIM for Coordination**: BIM plays a vital role in both quality control and commissioning. The digital model provides a 3D representation of the building and its systems, allowing project teams to detect potential issues before construction begins. During commissioning, the BIM model serves as a reference for verifying that systems are installed correctly and are functioning as designed.
- **BIM for Documentation**: BIM also helps streamline the documentation process during commissioning. All data related to equipment specifications, system settings, and performance testing can be stored and accessed in the BIM model, ensuring that all required information is readily available.

### B. IoT and Smart Building Systems

- **Real-Time Monitoring**: The Internet of Things (IoT) allows building systems to be monitored in real-time, enabling the early detection of performance issues during both quality control and commissioning. IoT-enabled sensors collect data on temperature, humidity, air quality, and energy usage, providing valuable insights into system performance.
- **Automation**: Many smart buildings incorporate automation technologies that allow systems to self-adjust for optimal performance. During commissioning, these systems can be tested and fine-tuned for maximum efficiency.

## C. Drones and Robotics

- **Drones**: Drones equipped with cameras and sensors can be used to perform inspections of building facades, roofs, and hard-to-reach areas. They can capture real-time images and video, which can then be analysed for quality control purposes.
- **Robotics**: In some projects, robotics is used for tasks such as precise calibration, testing, and even system adjustments during commissioning. This allows for faster, more accurate performance checks.

## 5. Final Walkthroughs and Handover

The **final walkthrough** is a critical step in both quality control and commissioning. This is when the building owner, project manager, contractors, and other key stakeholders review the entire project to ensure that everything is in place and functioning as expected.

### A. Final Punch List

During the final walkthrough, a **punch list** is created, which identifies any minor tasks or issues that need to be addressed before the building is handed over. The punch list may include tasks such as:

- Touch-ups on finishes or paint
- Adjustments to system settings or equipment
- Minor repairs or tweaks to functionality

### B. Client Handover

After all issues identified during the final walkthrough have been resolved, the building is formally handed over to the client. This includes providing all relevant **documentation**, such as warranties, user manuals, and maintenance schedules for the systems installed in the building.

### Conclusion

Quality control and commissioning are integral to the successful completion of any building project. Through comprehensive testing, verification, and optimization, these processes ensure that a building meets its design specifications, performs as expected, and is ready for occupancy. By integrating modern technologies like **BIM**, **IoT**, and **real-time monitoring systems**, the commissioning process is more efficient, accurate, and reliable than ever before.

As buildings become smarter, more energy-efficient, and increasingly automated, the role of quality control and commissioning will only grow in importance. With ongoing advancements in technology, the future of these processes will continue to evolve, enabling project teams to deliver buildings that are not only high-performing but also sustainable, cost-effective, and aligned with the needs of their occupants.

# CHAPTER FIFTEEN

# The Future of Integrated Design

The field of architecture and building design has evolved dramatically over the past few decades. With advancements in technology, shifts in sustainability priorities, and changes in how buildings are managed and used, the future of **integrated design**—especially when it comes to **Mechanical, Electrical, Plumbing (MEPF), fire protection (F),** and architectural coordination—looks set to be incredibly exciting. Emerging technologies such as **Artificial Intelligence (AI), Building Information Modelling (BIM), Internet of Things (IoT),** and **automation** are not only reshaping how buildings are designed and constructed but also how they are operated and maintained throughout their lifecycle.

This chapter explores the future trajectory of integrated design, focusing on the **technological innovations, industry trends,** and **new design methodologies** that will continue to shape the construction industry. From **sustainability** and **automation** to **artificial intelligence** and **prefabrication,** integrated design will be influenced by a variety of external and internal factors that drive performance, efficiency, and occupant satisfaction.

**1. The Evolution of Integrated Design and the Increasing Role of Technology**

In the past, the architectural, engineering, and construction (AEC) industries have been relatively siloed, with different professionals working on their own aspects of a project without much collaboration or integration. However, over the past few decades, **integrated design** has become a dominant practice in modern architecture. The rise of **collaborative design** techniques, particularly in the context of MEPF systems, has paved the way for buildings that are more energy-efficient, sustainable, and cost-effective.

**Key milestones in the evolution of integrated design:**

- **Early Collaboration**: Initially, integrated design began with a push for collaboration between architects, engineers, and contractors. This included using tools like **BIM** to ensure that various systems were integrated early on, leading to fewer design conflicts during construction.
- **Sustainability and Green Building Certifications**: As sustainability became a higher priority, integrated design helped achieve goals such as **LEED, BREEAM**, and **IGBC** certifications. This focus ensured that all aspects of the building—from HVAC systems to lighting—worked together for energy efficiency, resource conservation, and occupant comfort.
- **Rise of Smart Buildings**: With the proliferation of **smart technologies**, including **IoT** devices, **sensors**, and **automated systems**, integrated design grew to encompass not only construction and design but also building performance management. Smart systems that can be controlled and optimized in real-time, along with ongoing monitoring, further enhanced integrated design.

As technology continues to advance, integrated design will expand to include even more sophisticated tools, software, and systems that will redefine how buildings are conceived, constructed, and managed.

**2. The Role of Artificial Intelligence (AI) and Machine Learning (ML)**

Artificial intelligence (AI) and machine learning (ML) are already making a significant impact in various industries, and the **AEC** sector is no exception. In integrated design, these technologies will have profound implications for everything from building design and construction to facility management and operations.

**A. AI in Design and Planning**

- **Generative Design**: AI algorithms can now be used to generate design solutions based on specific parameters and constraints. **Generative design** uses algorithms to create thousands of design alternatives, which can then be optimized for energy efficiency, structural performance, or cost-effectiveness. In the context of integrated MEPF systems, AI can help design systems that work together seamlessly, reducing conflicts and maximizing performance.
- **Parametric Design and Simulation**: AI will increasingly work in conjunction with **parametric design tools** (e.g., Rhino, Grasshopper)

to simulate real-world performance under varying conditions. AI can suggest design improvements based on performance simulations, helping architects and engineers make better decisions about MEPF system sizing, energy use, and environmental impact.

## B. AI for Predictive Maintenance and Building Optimization

- **Predictive Analytics for Building Performance**: AI can analyse vast amounts of real-time data from sensors embedded in building systems (e.g., HVAC, plumbing, electrical) to predict when equipment is likely to fail or needs maintenance. This helps prevent costly breakdowns and downtime by enabling proactive intervention.
- **Energy Optimization**: AI and ML algorithms can continuously optimize building systems for **energy efficiency** by analysing patterns in occupancy, temperature, humidity, and other factors. AI-enabled systems can adjust HVAC settings or lighting based on occupancy patterns, improving energy performance and reducing operational costs.

## C. Automation and Robotics in Construction

- **Robotic Construction**: Automation in construction is becoming increasingly common. **Robotic systems** can help with tasks such as bricklaying, welding, and even complex installations like HVAC or electrical systems. These systems reduce human error, increase precision, and accelerate construction timelines.
- **3D Printing**: The use of **3D printing** in construction is gaining momentum. **3D printing of building materials** such as concrete, steel, or polymer-based composites will allow architects and engineers to experiment with new building forms that were previously difficult or costly to construct.

AI and automation will continue to reshape integrated design by making the construction process more efficient and error-free, while also optimizing the building's operational performance after construction is complete.

**3. The Role of Building Information Modelling (BIM) in the Future of Integrated Design**

Building Information Modelling (BIM) has been a game-changer in the AEC industry, enabling better collaboration and integration between architects, engineers, and contractors. However, as the **digital transformation** continues, BIM is evolving and expanding to include **4D, 5D,** and **6D BIM**—with more advanced features related to time, cost, and operational management.

**A. 4D, 5D, and 6D BIM**

- **4D BIM (Time):** In the future, BIM will include detailed scheduling and sequencing of construction activities. With **4D BIM,** project teams can visualize the construction process and simulate potential delays or conflicts in construction schedules before they occur.
- **5D BIM (Cost): 5D BIM** integrates cost data into the BIM model, allowing project teams to track project budgets in real-time, optimize material usage, and identify cost-saving opportunities early in the project.
- **6D BIM (Operations and Maintenance):** 6D BIM extends BIM to cover building operations and maintenance after construction. By linking BIM to **facility management software** and integrating it with **IoT devices,** the building can be continuously monitored and optimized throughout its lifecycle, ensuring it operates efficiently and reducing long-term operational costs.

**B. BIM for Sustainability**

BIM plays a critical role in sustainability and green building certification processes. The integration of **energy modelling** within BIM allows for early-stage analysis of a building's energy use and performance. Tools within BIM, such as **energy simulation** and **daylighting analysis,** can optimize the design of MEPF systems for energy efficiency, which is crucial for achieving green building certifications such as LEED or BREEAM.

In the future, BIM will be even more critical in assessing a building's environmental impact, helping design teams to achieve **carbon neutrality, net-zero energy,** and other sustainability goals.

**4. The Internet of Things (IoT) and Smart Buildings**

The Internet of Things (IoT) connects physical devices, systems, and sensors to the internet, enabling them to communicate, share data, and be controlled remotely. In smart buildings, IoT technologies are essential for integrating and optimizing various building systems.

### A. IoT in MEPF System Integration

- **Real-Time Data Monitoring**: IoT sensors can be embedded in MEPF systems such as HVAC, lighting, and plumbing to collect data in real time. These sensors provide valuable insights into system performance, helping building managers and engineers monitor energy consumption, air quality, and system efficiency.
- **Energy Management: Smart meters** and **energy management systems** (EMS) use IoT technology to track energy usage and provide real-time data on building performance. These systems enable **demand-response strategies**, where energy consumption is automatically adjusted based on grid conditions, time of day, or occupancy.

### B. IoT for Occupant Comfort and Safety

- **Smart HVAC and Lighting Systems**: Occupants can use **smart thermostats** and **lighting controls** to personalize their environment. These systems adjust automatically based on occupancy, external weather conditions, or individual preferences.
- **Building Security: Smart security systems**, including biometric access, facial recognition, and surveillance cameras connected via IoT, enhance the security of smart buildings.

### C. Predictive Maintenance with IoT

- **Remote Diagnostics**: IoT-enabled devices can monitor the performance of MEPF systems and identify issues such as potential failures or inefficiencies. This information is sent to building managers or maintenance teams, enabling them to address problems before they escalate.
- **Asset Tracking and Management**: IoT technology can also be used to track building assets such as HVAC units, pumps, and lighting fixtures, ensuring they are maintained and replaced on time to avoid system failures.

### 5. Sustainability and the Future of Integrated Design

Sustainability will continue to be a driving force in the future of integrated design. As the effects of climate change become more apparent, the construction industry will be tasked with building **green**, **energy-efficient**, and **carbon-neutral** buildings.

**A. The Path to Net-Zero Buildings**

- **Energy Efficiency**: One of the most significant trends in integrated design is the push toward **net-zero buildings**, which consume only as much energy as they produce. This requires the integration of renewable energy sources like solar and wind power, along with high-efficiency MEPF systems and **smart energy management**.
- **Carbon-Neutral Design**: The future of integrated design will include carbon-neutral buildings that offset their carbon emissions by incorporating green energy systems and sustainable construction materials. The goal is to create buildings that not only minimize their environmental impact but also contribute to environmental restoration.

**B. Circular Economy in Building Design**

- **Material Reuse**: The concept of a **circular economy**—where materials are reused, recycled, and repurposed—is gaining traction in the construction industry. Integrated design will increasingly prioritize **sustainable materials**, reduce waste, and incorporate **building systems** that can be deconstructed and reused at the end of a building's life cycle.
- **Building as a Service**: The future may also see the rise of the "**building as a service**" model, where building systems are maintained, upgraded, and reused over time, minimizing the need for new resources and reducing the building's environmental footprint.

**Conclusion**

The future of integrated design is bright, shaped by **advancements in technology**, a growing focus on **sustainability**, and a more collaborative approach across the **architecture**, **engineering**, and **construction** industries. Technologies like **AI**, **BIM**, **IoT**, and **automation** will continue to drive innovation, enabling smarter, more energy-efficient buildings that meet the evolving needs of both occupants and the planet.

As we look forward, the integration of **smart technologies**, the push for **sustainability**, and the constant evolution of building systems will be key to creating a built environment that is more **resilient**, **efficient**, and **adaptive** to the challenges of the future.

Integrated design is no longer just about making buildings that work efficiently; it's about designing spaces that improve the **quality of life** for their occupants while also contributing to a **sustainable future** for the planet.